Restricted Congruences in Computing

Restricted Congruences in Computing

Khodakhast Bibak

CRC Press
Taylor & Francis Group
Boca Raton London New York

CRC Press is an imprint of the
Taylor & Francis Group, an **informa** business

First edition published 2021
by CRC Press
6000 Broken Sound Parkway NW, Suite 300, Boca Raton, FL 33487-2742

and by CRC Press
2 Park Square, Milton Park, Abingdon, Oxon, OX14 4RN

© 2021 Taylor & Francis Group, LLC
CRC Press is an imprint of Taylor & Francis Group, LLC

Library of Congress Cataloging-in-Publication Data
Names: Bibak, Khodakhast, author.
Title: Restricted congruences in computing / Khodakhast Bibak.
Description: First edition. | Boca Raton : CRC Press, 2021. | Includes
    bibliographical references and index.
Identifiers: LCCN 2020019044 (print) | LCCN 2020019045 (ebook) | ISBN
    9780367496036 (hardback) | ISBN 9781003047179 (ebook)
Subjects: LCSH: Congruences (Geometry) | Computer science--Mathematics.
Classification: LCC QA608 .B48 2021 (print) | LCC QA608 (ebook) | DDC
    512.7/2--dc23
LC record available at https://lccn.loc.gov/2020019044
LC ebook record available at https://lccn.loc.gov/2020019045

ISBN: 978-0-367-49603-6 (hbk)
ISBN: 978-0-367-49731-6 (pbk)
ISBN: 978-1-003-04717-9 (ebk)

Typeset in Minion
by Nova Techset Private Limited, Bengaluru & Chennai, India

Visit the Taylor & Francis Web site at
http://www.taylorandfrancis.com

and the CRC Press Web site at
http://www.crcpress.com

To my beloved wife Azadeh

Contents

Preface

CONGRUENCES ARE UBIQUITOUS IN computer science, engineering, mathematics, and related areas. Therefore, studying (the number of) solutions of a congruence is a fundamental problem. But, there are many scenarios in which we are interested in only a subset of the solutions; in other words, there are some *restrictions* on the solutions. What do we know about these types of congruences, their solutions, and their applications? As the first book of its kind, *Restricted Congruences in Computing* systematically studies congruences with various restrictions and also discusses their applications in many areas with a focus on computing.

CHAPTER 1

Introduction

1.1 MOTIVATION

Let $a_1, \ldots, a_k, b, n \in \mathbb{Z}, n \geq 1$. A linear congruence in k unknowns $x_1, \ldots, x_k$ is of the form

$$a_1 x_1 + \cdots + a_k x_k \equiv b \pmod{n}. \qquad (1.1.1)$$

Congruences are ubiquitous in computer science, engineering, mathematics, and related areas. They have a wide range of applications, for example, in

- cryptography and information security;
- universal hashing;
- parallel computing;
- quantum computing;
- data structures and algorithms;
- computational complexity;
- information theory and coding theory;
- DNA-based data storage systems;

- game theory;

- signal processing;

- geometry and physics (like string theory and QFT);

- the Subset-Sum Problem;

- discrete mathematics and number theory.

Research on congruences has also led to other seminal applications. For example, Levenshtein in his fundamental paper [121], as part of his generalization of the Varshamov–Tenengolts code (where congruences play a major role), also introduced the *edit distance* (also known as the *Levenshtein distance*), which is the most important measure of similarity of two strings (words), and is defined as the minimum number of character deletions, insertions, or substitutions required to transform one string (word) into the other. The edit distance and its generalizations/variants have many important applications in natural language processing and computational biology.

Therefore, developing techniques for finding (the number of) solutions of congruences and their variants is an important problem, and this book is devoted to studying such problems and their applications.

By a solution of (1.1.1) we mean an ordered k-tuple of integers modulo n, denoted by $\langle x_1, \ldots, x_k \rangle$, that satisfies (1.1.1). Let $(u_1, \ldots, u_m)$ denote the greatest common divisor (gcd) of $u_1, \ldots, u_m \in \mathbb{Z}$. The following classical result, proved by D. N. Lehmer [116], gives the number of solutions of this congruence.

Proposition 1.1.1. *Let $a_1, \ldots, a_k, b, n \in \mathbb{Z}$, $n \geq 1$. The linear congruence $a_1 x_1 + \cdots + a_k x_k \equiv b \pmod{n}$ has a solution $\langle x_1, \ldots, x_k \rangle \in \mathbb{Z}_n^k$ if and only if $\ell \mid b$, where $\ell = (a_1, \ldots, a_k, n)$. Furthermore, if this condition is satisfied, then there are ℓn^{k-1} solutions.*

Though Proposition 1.1.1 is elementary and quite easy to prove, it is a fundamental result that has stimulated a great deal of research in computer science, mathematics, and related areas. Note that Proposition 1.1.1 considers all solutions with $x_i \in \mathbb{Z}_n$, where $\mathbb{Z}_n = \{0, \ldots, n-1\}$. *But, there are many other scenarios in which the x_i are in a specified subset of $\mathbb{Z}_n$; in these scenarios we say that there are restrictions on the x_i.* What are the motivations for imposing restrictions, and what can we say about the number of solutions of congruences in the presence of restrictions?

In this book, we systematically study congruences with various restrictions and also discuss their applications in many areas, with a focus on computing. We remark that there are several other books that also consider congruences and their applications, such as [57, 178], but what fundamentally distinguishes our book from the aforementioned books is that in almost all congruences considered here, some restrictions have been imposed on their solutions. These restrictions are quite natural and have led to surprising applications. Though these congruences are widespread in the literature, there is no book on these congruences. This book is the first of its kind that is devoted to the restricted congruences and their applications [19, 29, 30, 20, 21, 22, 23, 25, 24, 26, 27, 28].

1.2 OVERVIEW OF THE BOOK

A brief overview of each chapter is as follows. In Chapter 2, we introduce a wide variety of tools and techniques that are needed for studying the restricted congruences and their applications.

In Chapter 3, we study the number of solutions of the congruence (1.1.1) when the greatest common divisors (gcds) of the coordinates x_i and the modulus n are certain numbers. More formally, we study solutions when $(x_i, n) = t_i$ $(1 \le i \le k)$, where $t_1, \ldots, t_k$ are given positive divisors of n. To see how general the problem is, note that when all gcds are equal to 1 (that is, when $t_i = 1$), the problem is asking for the solutions of the congruence (1.1.1) when $x_i \in \mathbb{Z}_n^*$, where $\mathbb{Z}_n^*$ is the multiplicative group of integers modulo n. The problem is very well motivated and has intriguing applications in several areas of mathematics, computer science, and physics, and there is promise for more applications/implications in these or other directions. Some of these applications are discussed in the next chapters.

Universal hashing, discovered by Carter and Wegman in 1979, has many important applications in computer science. MMH* (Multilinear Modular Hashing) is a well-known universal hash function family. In Chapter 4, we connect restricted linear congruences to universal hash functions, which is a novel idea and could be also of independent interest. We introduce generalizations/variants of MMH* and, using the restricted congruences studied in Chapter 3, investigate their universality. Finally, as an application of our results, we propose an authentication code with secrecy scheme.

Graphs embedded into surfaces have many important applications, in particular, in combinatorics, geometry, and physics. For example, ribbon graphs and their counting is of great interest in string theory and quantum field theory (QFT). For counting ribbon graphs, we need to know the number of surface-kernel epimorphisms from a co-compact Fuchsian group to a cyclic group. In Chapter 5, using the restricted congruences studied in Chapter 3, we give an explicit and practical formula for the number of such epimorphisms. As a consequence, we obtain an 'equivalent' form of Harvey's famous theorem on the cyclic groups of automorphisms of compact Riemann surfaces.

Another restriction of potential interest is imposing the condition that all x_i are *distinct*. We call such congruences *alldiff congruences*. Quite surprisingly, the number of solutions of this type of congruence was first considered, in a special case, by Schönemann in 1839 [174], but his result seems to have been overlooked. In Chapter 6, we generalize Schönemann's theorem via a graph theoretic method, which may be also of independent interest. We also consider unweighted alldiff congruences and, using properties of Ramanujan sums and of the discrete Fourier transform of arithmetic functions, give an explicit formula for the number of their solutions. We even go further and discuss applications/connections to several combinatorial problems.

In Chapter 7, we discuss applications of the previous results to coding theory. Specifically, we connect an important class of codes, namely, the Varshamov–Tenengolts codes, to alldiff congruences studied in Chapter 6. As an application, we derive explicit formulas for the size of the Varshamov–Tenengolts codes and also for the number of codewords in these codes with Hamming weight k, that is, with exactly k 1s. This approach provides a general framework and gives new insight into these problems, which might lead to further work.

In Chapter 8, we study the congruences with the restrictions $x_i \in \{0, 1\}$, that is, the congruences with binary solutions. Putting it in coding theory language, we introduce the Binary Linear Congruence Code (BLCC), which includes several well-known classes of deletion/insertion correcting codes as special cases. For example, the Helberg code, the Levenshtein code, the Varshamov–Tenengolts code, and most variants of these codes including most of those that have been recently used in studying DNA-based data storage systems are all special cases of BLCC. We give an explicit formula for the weight enumerator of BLCC, which in turn gives explicit formulas for the weight enumerators and so the sizes of all the aforementioned codes. As another application, we derive an explicit formula for the number of binary solutions of an *arbitrary* linear congruence. These results might have more applications/implications in information theory, computer science, and mathematics.

Congruences have been also used in many other areas. For example, congruences with binary solutions (which will be studied in Chapter 8) have interesting applications in database security and pseudo-telepathy games in quantum computing. In Chapter 9, we discuss applications of congruences to parallel computing, artificial intelligence, computational biology, and the Subset-Sum Problem.

In Chapter 10, we consider an important application of quadratic congruences in studying Ramanujan graphs and the famous Golomb–Welch conjecture in coding theory. The long-standing Golomb–Welch conjecture states that there are no perfect Lee codes for spheres of radius greater than 1 and dimension greater than 2. Resolving this conjecture has been one of the main motivations for studying perfect and quasi-perfect Lee codes. It has been shown that for every prime number $p > 5$ such that $p \equiv \pm 5$ (mod 12), the Cayley graph $\mathcal{G}_p = \mathrm{Cay}(\mathbb{Z}_p[i], S_2)$, where S_2 is the set of units of $\mathbb{Z}_p[i]$, induces a 2-quasi-perfect Lee code over $\mathbb{Z}_p^m$, where $m = 2\lfloor \frac{p}{4} \rfloor$. In Chapter 10, we prove that the Cayley graph $\mathcal{G}_p = \mathrm{Cay}(\mathbb{Z}_p[i], S_2)$ is a Ramanujan graph for every prime p such that $p \equiv 3$ (mod 4). This solves a conjecture from [40]. Our proof techniques may motivate more work in the interactions between spectral graph theory, character theory, and coding theory, and may provide new ideas towards the Golomb–Welch conjecture.

CHAPTER 2

The Restricted Congruences Toolbox

I N ORDER TO STUDY THE RESTRICTED congruences and their applications, we need a wide variety of tools and techniques from several areas. In this chapter, we introduce these tools. Throughout the book we let $\mathbb{Z}_n = \{0, \ldots, n - 1\}$. Two integers are said to be *coprime* (*relatively prime*) if their greatest common divisor (gcd) is 1. The set of integers from $\mathbb{Z}_n$ coprime to n form a group under multiplication modulo n, called the *multiplicative group of integers modulo n*, and denoted by $\mathbb{Z}_n^*$. We use $(a_1, \ldots, a_k)$ and $\mathrm{lcm}(a_1, \ldots, a_k)$ to denote, respectively, the greatest common divisor and the least common multiple of integers $a_1, \ldots, a_k$, and write $\langle a_1, \ldots, a_k \rangle$ for an ordered k-tuple of integers. Also, for $a \in \mathbb{Z} \setminus \{0\}$ and a prime p, we use the notation $p^r \mid\mid a$ if $p^r \mid a$ and $p^{r+1} \nmid a$. For a set $\mathcal{X}$, we write $x \leftarrow \mathcal{X}$ to denote that x is chosen uniformly at random from $\mathcal{X}$. We also use $\mathbf{0}$ to denote the vector of all zeroes.

2.1 RAMANUJAN SUMS

Let $e(x) = \exp(2\pi i x)$ be the complex exponential with period 1. It satisfies for any $m, n \in \mathbb{Z}$ with $n \geq 1$,

$$\sum_{j=1}^{n} e\left(\frac{jm}{n}\right) = \begin{cases} n, & \text{if } n \mid m, \\ 0, & \text{if } n \nmid m. \end{cases} \tag{2.1.1}$$

More generally, we can prove the following result.

Lemma 2.1.1. *Let n be a positive integer and x be a real number. Then, we have*

$$\sum_{m=1}^{n} e(mx) = \begin{cases} n, & \text{if } x \in \mathbb{Z}, \\ \frac{\sin(nx\pi)}{\sin(x\pi)} e\left(\frac{(n+1)x}{2}\right), & \text{if } x \in \mathbb{R} \setminus \mathbb{Z}. \end{cases} \tag{2.1.2}$$

Proof. When $x \in \mathbb{Z}$, the result is clear because in this case $e(x) = e(mx) = 1$. So, we let $x \in \mathbb{R} \setminus \mathbb{Z}$. Since $e(x) \neq 1$, summing the geometric progression gives

$$\begin{aligned}
\sum_{m=1}^{n} e(mx) &= \frac{e(x)\,(1 - e(nx))}{1 - e(x)} \\
&= \frac{e\left(\frac{x}{2}\right)(1 - e(nx))}{e\left(\frac{-x}{2}\right)(1 - e(x))} \\
&= \frac{e\left(\frac{x}{2}\right) - e\left(\frac{(2n+1)x}{2}\right)}{e\left(\frac{-x}{2}\right) - e\left(\frac{x}{2}\right)} \\
&= \frac{e\left(\frac{-nx}{2}\right) - e\left(\frac{nx}{2}\right)}{e\left(\frac{-x}{2}\right) - e\left(\frac{x}{2}\right)} e\left(\frac{(n+1)x}{2}\right) \\
&= \frac{-2i\sin(nx\pi)}{-2i\sin(x\pi)} e\left(\frac{(n+1)x}{2}\right) \\
&= \frac{\sin(nx\pi)}{\sin(x\pi)} e\left(\frac{(n+1)x}{2}\right).
\end{aligned}$$

$\square$

For integers m and n with $n \geq 1$, the quantity

$$c_n(m) = \sum_{\substack{j=1 \\ (j,n)=1}}^{n} e\left(\frac{jm}{n}\right) \tag{2.1.3}$$

is called a *Ramanujan sum*. It is the sum of the mth powers of the primitive nth roots of unity, and is also denoted by $c(m, n)$ in the literature. Even though the Ramanujan sum $c_n(m)$ is defined as a sum of some complex numbers, it is integer-valued (see Theorem 2.1.2). From (2.1.3), it is clear that $c_n(-m) = c_n(m)$.

Ramanujan sums and some of their properties were certainly known before Ramanujan's paper [157], as Ramanujan himself declared; nonetheless, probably the reason that these sums bear Ramanujan's name is that 'Ramanujan was the first to appreciate the importance of the sum and to use it systematically', according to Hardy (see [66] for a discussion about this).

Ramanujan sums have important applications in additive number theory, for example, in the context of the Hardy–Littlewood circle method, Waring's problem, and sieve theory (see, e.g., [145, 148, 202] and the references therein). As a major result in this direction, one can mention Vinogradov's theorem (in its proof, Ramanujan sums play a key role) stating that every sufficiently large odd integer is the sum of three primes, and so every sufficiently large even integer is the sum of four primes (see, e.g., [148, Ch. 8]). Ramanujan sums have also interesting applications in cryptography [28, 173], coding theory [24, 71], combinatorics [26, 137], graph theory [62, 132], signal processing [197, 198], and physics [21, 154].

Clearly, $c_n(0) = \varphi(n)$, where $\varphi(n)$ is *Euler's totient function*. Also, by Theorem 2.1.2, $c_n(1) = \mu(n)$, where $\mu(n)$ is the *Möbius function* defined by

$$\mu(n) = \begin{cases} 1, & \text{if } n = 1, \\ 0, & \text{if } n \text{ is not square-free,} \\ (-1)^\kappa, & \text{if } n \text{ is the product of } \kappa \text{ distinct primes.} \end{cases} \tag{2.1.4}$$

The following theorem, attributed to Kluyver [103], gives an explicit formula for $c_n(m)$.

Theorem 2.1.2. *For integers m and n, with $n \geq 1$,*

$$c_n(m) = \sum_{d \mid (m,n)} \mu\left(\frac{n}{d}\right) d. \qquad (2.1.5)$$

Thus, $c_n(m)$ can be easily computed provided n can be factored efficiently. One should compare (2.1.5) with the formula

$$\varphi(n) = \sum_{d \mid n} \mu\left(\frac{n}{d}\right) d. \qquad (2.1.6)$$

The following well-known result gives equivalent defining formulas for a related function, namely, *Jordan's totient function* $J_k(n)$ (see, e.g., [135, pp. 13–14]).

Lemma 2.1.3. *Let n, k be positive integers. Then,*

$$J_k(n) = \sum_{d \mid n} d^k \mu\left(\frac{n}{d}\right) = n^k \prod_{p \mid n}\left(1 - \frac{1}{p^k}\right), \qquad (2.1.7)$$

where the left summation is taken over all positive divisors d of n, and the right product is taken over all prime divisors p of n.

By applying the Möbius inversion formula, Theorem 2.1.2 yields the following property: For $m, n \geq 1$,

$$\sum_{d \mid n} c_d(m) = \begin{cases} n, & \text{if } n \mid m, \\ 0, & \text{if } n \nmid m. \end{cases} \qquad (2.1.8)$$

The case $m = 1$ of (2.1.8) gives the *characteristic property* of the Möbius function:

$$\sum_{d \mid n} \mu(d) = \begin{cases} 1, & \text{if } n = 1, \\ 0, & \text{if } n > 1. \end{cases} \qquad (2.1.9)$$

Note that Theorem 2.1.2 has several other important consequences.

Corollary 2.1.4. *Ramanujan sums enjoy the following properties:*

(i) *For fixed $m \in \mathbb{Z}$, the function $n \mapsto c_n(m)$ is multiplicative, that is, if $(n_1, n_2) = 1$, then $c_{n_1 n_2}(m) = c_{n_1}(m) c_{n_2}(m)$. (Note that the function $m \mapsto c_n(m)$ is multiplicative for a fixed n if and only if $\mu(n) = 1$.) Furthermore, for every prime power p^r $(r \geq 1)$,*

$$c_{p^r}(m) = \begin{cases} p^r - p^{r-1}, & \text{if } p^r \mid m, \\ -p^{r-1}, & \text{if } p^{r-1} \parallel m, \\ 0, & \text{if } p^{r-1} \nmid m. \end{cases} \qquad (2.1.10)$$

(ii) *The sum $c_n(m)$ is integer-valued.*

(iii) *The sum $c_n(m)$ is an even function of m (mod n), that is, $c_n(m) = c_n((m, n))$, for every m, n.*

The *von Sterneck number* [204] is defined by

$$\Phi(m, n) = \frac{\varphi(n)}{\varphi\left(\frac{n}{(m,n)}\right)} \mu\left(\frac{n}{(m, n)}\right). \qquad (2.1.11)$$

A crucial fact in studying Ramanujan sums and their applications is that they coincide with the von Sterneck numbers. This result is known as *von Sterneck's formula* and is attributed to Kluyver [103].

Theorem 2.1.5. *For integers m and n, with n ≥ 1, we have*

$$\Phi(m, n) = c_n(m). \tag{2.1.12}$$

Ramanujan sums satisfy several important *orthogonality properties*. One of them is the following identity.

Theorem 2.1.6. [43] *If $n \geq 1$, $d_1 \mid n$, and $d_2 \mid n$, then we have*

$$\sum_{d \mid n} c_{d_1}\left(\frac{n}{d}\right) c_d\left(\frac{n}{d_2}\right) = \begin{cases} n, & \text{if } d_1 = d_2, \\ 0, & \text{if } d_1 \neq d_2. \end{cases} \tag{2.1.13}$$

We close this section by mentioning that, very recently, Fowler et al. [66] showed that many properties of Ramanujan sums can be deduced (with very short proofs!) using the theory of *supercharacters* (from group theory), developed by Diaconis and André in the early 2000s (see references in [66]).

2.2 SOME USEFUL IDENTITIES

We also need the following useful and interesting identities.

Lemma 2.2.1. *Let n be a positive integer and m be a non-negative integer. We have*

$$\prod_{j=1}^{n} \left(1 - z e^{2\pi i j m/n}\right) = (1 - z^{\frac{n}{d}})^d,$$

where $d = (m, n)$.

Proof. It is well-known that [185, p. 167]

$$1 - z^n = \prod_{j=1}^{n} \left(1 - z e^{2\pi i j/n}\right).$$

Now, letting $d = (m, n)$, we obtain

$$\prod_{j=1}^{n} \left(1 - ze^{2\pi ijm/n}\right) = \prod_{j=1}^{n} \left(1 - ze^{2\pi ij\frac{m/d}{n/d}}\right)$$

$$= \left(\prod_{j=1}^{n/d} \left(1 - ze^{2\pi ij\frac{m/d}{n/d}}\right)\right)^{d}$$

$$\stackrel{(\frac{m}{d},\frac{n}{d})=1}{=} \left(\prod_{j=1}^{n/d} \left(1 - ze^{\frac{2\pi ij}{n/d}}\right)\right)^{d} = (1 - z^{\frac{n}{d}})^{d}.$$

$\square$

Similarly, we can prove the following lemma.

Lemma 2.2.2. *Let n be a positive integer and m be a non-negative integer. We have*

$$\prod_{j=1}^{n} \left(z - e^{2\pi ijm/n}\right) = (z^{\frac{n}{d}} - 1)^{d},$$

where $d = (m, n)$.

By changing z to $-z$ and using the binomial theorem, Lemma 2.2.1 gives the following.

Corollary 2.2.3. *Let n be a positive integer and m, k be non-negative integers. The coefficient of z^{k} in*

$$\prod_{j=1}^{n} \left(1 + ze^{2\pi ijm/n}\right)$$

is $(-1)^{k+\frac{kd}{n}} \binom{\frac{d}{n}}{\frac{kd}{n}}$, where $d = (m, n)$.

2.3 THE DISCRETE FOURIER TRANSFORM

A function $f : \mathbb{Z} \to \mathbb{C}$ is called *periodic* with period n (also called *n-periodic* or *periodic* modulo n) if $f(m + n) = f(m)$, for every $m \in \mathbb{Z}$. In this case f is determined by the finite vector $(f(1), \ldots, f(n))$. From (2.1.3) it is clear that $c_n(m)$ is a periodic function of m with period n.

We define the *discrete Fourier transform* (DFT) of an n-periodic function f as the function $\widehat{f} = \mathcal{F}(f)$, given by

$$\widehat{f}(b) = \sum_{j=1}^{n} f(j) e\left(\frac{-bj}{n}\right) \quad (b \in \mathbb{Z}). \tag{2.3.1}$$

The standard representation of f is obtained from the Fourier representation $\widehat{f}$ by

$$f(b) = \frac{1}{n} \sum_{j=1}^{n} \widehat{f}(j) e\left(\frac{bj}{n}\right) \quad (b \in \mathbb{Z}), \tag{2.3.2}$$

which is the *inverse discrete Fourier transform* (IDFT) (see, e.g., [145, p. 109]).

The *Cauchy convolution* of the n-periodic functions f_1 and f_2 is the n-periodic function $f_1 \otimes f_2$ defined by

$$(f_1 \otimes f_2)(m) = \sum_{\substack{1 \le x_1, x_2 \le n \\ x_1 + x_2 \equiv m \pmod{n}}} f_1(x_1) f_2(x_2) = \sum_{x=1}^{n} f_1(x) f_2(m - x) \quad (m \in \mathbb{Z}).$$

It is well known that

$$\widehat{f_1 \otimes f_2} = \widehat{f_1} \widehat{f_2},$$

with pointwise multiplication. More generally, if $f_1, \ldots, f_k$ are n-periodic functions, then

$$\mathcal{F}(f_1 \otimes \cdots \otimes f_k) = \mathcal{F}(f_1) \cdots \mathcal{F}(f_k). \tag{2.3.3}$$

For $t \mid n$, let $\varrho_{n,t}$ be the n-periodic function defined for every $m \in \mathbb{Z}$ by

$$\varrho_{n,t}(m) = \begin{cases} 1, & \text{if } (m,n) = t, \\ 0, & \text{if } (m,n) \neq t. \end{cases}$$

We will need the next two results. The first one is a direct consequence of the definitions.

Theorem 2.3.1. *For every* $t \mid n$,

$$\widehat{\varrho_{n,t}}(m) = c_{\frac{n}{t}}(m) \quad (m \in \mathbb{Z});$$

in particular, the Ramanujan sum $m \mapsto c_n(m)$ *is the DFT of the function* $m \mapsto \varrho_{n,1}(m)$.

As already mentioned in Corollary 2.1.4(iii), a function $f : \mathbb{Z} \to \mathbb{C}$ is called n-even, or even modulo n, if $f(m) = f((m,n))$ for every $m \in \mathbb{Z}$. Clearly, if a function f is n-even, then it is n-periodic. The Ramanujan sum $m \mapsto c_n(m)$ is an example of an n-even function.

Theorem 2.3.2. **[195, Prop. 2]** *If* f *is an* n-even function, then

$$\widehat{f}(m) = \sum_{d \mid n} f(d) c_{\frac{n}{d}}(m) \quad (m \in \mathbb{Z}).$$

Proof. Group the terms of (2.3.1) according to the values $d = (m,n)$, taking into account the definition of n-even functions. $\square$

2.4 UNIVERSAL HASHING AND ITS VARIANTS

Let D and R be finite sets. Let H be a family of functions from domain D to range R. We say that H is a *universal* family of hash functions [41] if the probability, over a random choice of a hash function from H, that two distinct keys in D have the same hash value is at most $\frac{1}{|R|}$. That is, universal hashing captures the important property that distinct keys in D do not *collide* too often. Furthermore, we say that H is an ε-*almost-universal* (ε-AU) family of hash functions if the probability of collision is at most ε, for $\frac{1}{|R|} \le \varepsilon < 1$. In other words, an ε-AU family, for sufficiently small ε, is *close* to being universal; see Definition 2.4.1. Universal and almost-universal hash functions have many applications in algorithm design. For example, they have been used to provide efficient solutions for the dictionary problem in which the goal is to maintain a dynamic set that is updated using insert and delete operations using small space so that membership queries that ask if a certain element is in S can be answered quickly.

Motivated by applications to cryptography, a notion of Δ-universality was introduced [109, 162, 188]. Suppose that R is an Abelian group. We say that H is a Δ-*universal* family of hash functions if the probability, over a random $h \in H$, that two distinct keys in D hash to values that are distance b apart for any b in R is $\frac{1}{|R|}$. Note that the case $b = 0$ corresponds to universality. Furthermore, we say that H is ε-*almost-Δ-universal* (ε-AΔU) if this probability is at most ε, $\frac{1}{|R|} \le \varepsilon < 1$. We remark that ε-AΔU families have applications to message authentication. Informally, it is possible to design a message authentication scheme using ε-AΔU families such that two parties can exchange signed messages over an unreliable channel and the probability that an adversary can forge a valid signed message to be sent across the channel is at most ε [78]. Also, the well-known leftover hash lemma states that (almost) universal hash functions are good randomness extractors.

We say that H is a *strongly universal* family of hash functions [207] if the probability, over a random choice of a hash function from H, that two distinct keys x and y in D are mapped to a and b, respectively, is $\frac{1}{|R|^2}$. We say that H is ε-*almost-strongly-universal* (ε-ASU) if this probability is at most ε, $\frac{1}{|R|^2} \le \varepsilon < \frac{1}{|R|}$. We now provide a formal definition of the concepts just introduced as in [78].

Definition 2.4.1. Let H be a family of functions from a domain D to a range R. Let ε be a constant such that $\frac{1}{|R|} \leq \varepsilon < 1$. The following probabilities are taken over the random choice of hash function h from the set H.

- The family H is a *universal family of hash functions* if for any two distinct $x, y \in D$, we have $\Pr_{h \leftarrow H}[h(x) = h(y)] \leq \frac{1}{|R|}$. Also, H is an *ε-almost-universal (ε-AU) family of hash functions* if for any two distinct $x, y \in D$, we have $\Pr_{h \leftarrow H}[h(x) = h(y)] \leq \varepsilon$.

- Suppose that R is an Abelian group. The family H is a *Δ-universal family of hash functions* if for any two distinct $x, y \in D$ and all $b \in R$, we have $\Pr_{h \leftarrow H}[h(x) - h(y) = b] = \frac{1}{|R|}$, where '$-$' denotes the group subtraction operation. Also, H is an *ε-almost-Δ-universal (ε-AΔU) family of hash functions* if for any two distinct $x, y \in D$ and all $b \in R$, we have $\Pr_{h \leftarrow H}[h(x) - h(y) = b] \leq \varepsilon$.

- The family H is a *strongly universal family of hash functions* if for any two distinct $x, y \in D$ and all $a, b \in R$, we have $\Pr_{h \leftarrow H}[h(x) = a, \ h(y) = b] = \frac{1}{|R|^2}$. Also, H is an *ε-almost-strongly-universal (ε-ASU) family of hash functions* if for any two distinct $x, y \in D$ and all $a, b \in R$, we have $\Pr_{h \leftarrow H}[h(x) = a, \ h(y) = b] \leq \frac{\varepsilon}{|R|}$.

2.5 MULTILINEAR MODULAR HASHING

Here, we describe a well-known universal hash function family that was named MMH* (Multilinear Modular Hashing) by Halevi and Krawczyk [78]. Let p be a prime and k be a positive integer. Each hash function in the family MMH* takes as input a k-tuple, $\mathbf{m} = \langle m_1, \ldots, m_k \rangle \in \mathbb{Z}_p^k$. It computes the dot product of $\mathbf{m}$ with a fixed k-tuple $\mathbf{x} = \langle x_1, \ldots, x_k \rangle \in \mathbb{Z}_p^k$ and outputs this value modulo p.

Definition 2.5.1. Let p be a prime and k be a positive integer. The family MMH^* is defined as follows:

$$MMH^* := \{g_\mathbf{x} \ : \ \mathbb{Z}_p^k \to \mathbb{Z}_p \mid \mathbf{x} \in \mathbb{Z}_p^k\}, \qquad (2.5.1)$$

where

$$g_\mathbf{x}(\mathbf{m}) := \mathbf{m} \cdot \mathbf{x} \pmod{p} = \sum_{i=1}^{k} m_i x_i \pmod{p}, \qquad (2.5.2)$$

for any $\mathbf{x} = \langle x_1, \ldots, x_k \rangle \in \mathbb{Z}_p^k$ and any $\mathbf{m} = \langle m_1, \ldots, m_k \rangle \in \mathbb{Z}_p^k$.

The family MMH^* is widely attributed to Carter and Wegman [41], though it seems that Gilbert et al. [69] had already discovered it (but in the finite geometry setting). Halevi and Krawczyk [78], using the multiplicative inverse method, proved that MMH^* is a Δ-universal family of hash functions.

Theorem 2.5.2. [78, 119] *The family* MMH^* *is a* Δ-*universal family of hash functions.*

2.6 FUCHSIAN GROUPS AND HARVEY'S THEOREM

A *Fuchsian group* Γ is a finitely generated non-elementary discrete subgroup of $PSL(2, \mathbb{R})$, the group of orientation-preserving isometries of the hyperbolic plane $\mathbb{H}^2$. Fuchsian groups were first studied by Poincaré in 1882 in connection with the uniformization problem (later the uniformization theorem), and he called the groups Fuchsian after Lazarus Fuchs whose 1880 paper was a motivation for Poincaré to introduce this concept. By a classical result of Fricke and Klein (see, e.g., [212]), every such group Γ has a presentation in terms of the generators $a_1, b_1, \ldots, a_g, b_g$ (hyperbolic), $x_1, \ldots, x_k$ (elliptic), $y_1, \ldots, y_s$ (parabolic), and $z_1, \ldots, z_t$ (hyperbolic boundary elements) with the relations

$$x_1^{n_1} = \cdots = x_k^{n_k} = x_1 \cdots x_k y_1 \cdots y_s z_1 \cdots z_t [a_1, b_1] \cdots$$

$$[a_g, b_g] = 1, \qquad (2.6.1)$$

where $k, s, t, g \geq 0, n_i \geq 2$ $(1 \leq i \leq k)$, and $[a, b] = a^{-1}b^{-1}ab$. The integers $n_1, \ldots, n_k$ are called the *periods* of Γ, and g is called the *orbit genus*. The Fuchsian group Γ is determined, up to isomorphism, by the tuple $\langle g; n_1, \ldots, n_k; s; t \rangle$, which is referred to as the *signature* of Γ. If $k = 0$ (i.e., there are no periods), Γ is called a Fuchsian *surface group*. If $s = t = 0$, the group is called *co-compact* (or *F-group*, or *proper*). Some authors by a Fuchsian group mean a co-compact Fuchsian group. In this chapter, we only work with co-compact Fuchsian groups.

We denote by $\mathrm{Hom}(\Gamma, G)$ (resp., $\mathrm{Epi}(\Gamma, G)$) the set of homomorphisms (resp., epimorphisms) from a Fuchsian group Γ to a finite group G. There is much interest (with many applications) in combinatorics, geometry, algebra, and physics, in counting homomorphisms and epimorphisms from a Fuchsian group to a finite group. For example, Liebeck and Shalev [124, 125] obtained good estimates for $|\mathrm{Hom}(\Gamma, G)|$, where Γ is an arbitrary Fuchsian group and G is a symmetric group or an alternating group or a finite simple group.

An epimorphism from a Fuchsian group to a finite group with kernel a Fuchsian surface group is called *surface-kernel* (or *smooth*). Harvey proved that an epimorphism ϕ from a co-compact Fuchsian group Γ to a finite group G is surface-kernel if and only if it preserves the periods of Γ, that is, for every elliptic generator x_i $(1 \leq i \leq k)$ of order n_i, the order of $\phi(x_i)$ is precisely n_i. The above-mentioned equivalence appears in Harvey's influential 1966 paper [81] on the cyclic groups of automorphisms of compact Riemann surfaces. The main result of this paper is the following theorem that gives necessary and sufficient conditions for the existence of a surface-kernel epimorphism from a co-compact Fuchsian group to a cyclic group.

Theorem 2.6.1. [81] *Let Γ be a co-compact Fuchsian group with signature $(g; n_1, \ldots, n_k)$, and let $\mathfrak{n} := \mathrm{lcm}(n_1, \ldots, n_k)$. There is a surface-kernel epimorphism from Γ to $\mathbb{Z}_n$ if and only if the following conditions are satisfied:*

(i) $\operatorname{lcm}(n_1, \ldots, n_{i-1}, n_{i+1}, \ldots, n_k) = \mathfrak{n}$, *for all i;*

(ii) $\mathfrak{n} \mid n$, *and if* $g = 0$ *then* $\mathfrak{n} = n$;

(iii) $k \neq 1$, *and, if* $g = 0$ *then* $k > 2$;

(iv) *if* $\mathfrak{n}$ *is even then the number of periods* n_i *such that* $\mathfrak{n}/n_i$ *is odd is also even.*

By a result of Burnside [38], and of Greenberg [73], every finite group G acts as a group of automorphisms of a compact Riemann surface of genus at least 2. The *minimum genus* problem asks to find, for a given finite group G, the minimum genus of those compact Riemann surfaces on which G acts faithfully as a group of conformal automorphisms. Harvey [81], using Theorem 2.6.1, solved the minimum genus problem when G is the cyclic group $\mathbb{Z}_n$; in fact, he gave an explicit value for the minimum genus in terms of the prime factorization of n. Then, as a corollary, he obtained a famous result of Wiman [210] on the *maximum order* for an automorphism of a compact Riemann surface of genus γ by showing that this maximum order is $2(2\gamma + 1)$.

Harvey's paper [81] played a pioneering role in studying groups of automorphisms of compact Riemann surfaces and also has important applications in some other areas of mathematics like combinatorics. See, for example, the survey by Bujalance et al. [36] on the 'research inspired by Harvey's theorem', in which the authors describe many results about the actions of several classes of groups, including cyclic, Abelian, solvable, dihedral, along with the minimum genus and maximum order problems for these classes.

2.7 COUNTING EPIMORPHISMS VIA HOMOMORPHISMS

Generally, enumerating homomorphisms is easier than enumerating epimorphisms. Here, we prove a formula that connects the number of epimorphisms to the number of homomorphisms.

The classical version of the Möbius inversion formula states that if f and g are arithmetic functions satisfying $g(n) = \sum_{d \mid n} f(d)$, for every integer $n \geq 1$, then

$$f(n) = \sum_{d \mid n} \mu\left(\frac{n}{d}\right) g(d), \qquad (2.7.1)$$

for every integer $n \geq 1$. The Möbius function and Möbius inversion were studied for functions over locally finite partially ordered sets (posets) first by Weisner [208] and Hall [79], motivated by group theory problems. Later, Rota [163] extended this idea and put it in the context of combinatorics. Following the argument given by [79], we prove the following simple result.

Theorem 2.7.1. *Let Λ be a finitely generated group. Then,*

$$|\mathrm{Epi}(\Lambda, \mathbb{Z}_n)| = \sum_{d \mid n} \mu\left(\frac{n}{d}\right) |\mathrm{Hom}(\Lambda, \mathbb{Z}_d)|, \qquad (2.7.2)$$

where the summation is taken over all positive divisors d of n.

Proof. Clearly, for a finitely generated group Λ and a finite group G, we have

$$|\mathrm{Hom}(\Lambda, G)| = \sum_{H \leq G} |\mathrm{Epi}(\Lambda, H)|,$$

because every homomorphism from Λ to G induces a unique epimorphism from Λ to its image in G.

Taking $G = \mathbb{Z}_n$, and since the cyclic group $\mathbb{Z}_n$ has a unique subgroup $\mathbb{Z}_d$ for every positive divisor d of n and has no other subgroups, we get

$$|\mathrm{Hom}(\Lambda, \mathbb{Z}_n)| = \sum_{d \mid n} |\mathrm{Epi}(\Lambda, \mathbb{Z}_d)|.$$

Now, by applying the Möbius inversion formula (2.7.1), the theorem follows. □

2.8 GENERATING FUNCTIONS FOR GRAPH ENUMERATION

In order to study certain restricted congruences, we also need two formulas on graph enumeration. These formulas are in terms of the *deformed exponential function*, which is a special case of the *three-variable Rogers–Ramanujan function* defined in Definition 2.8.1. These functions have interesting applications in combinatorics, complex analysis, functional differential equations, and statistical mechanics (see [11, 108, 114, 127, 175, 182] and the references therein).

Definition 2.8.1. The *three-variable Rogers–Ramanujan function* is

$$R(\alpha, \beta, q) = \sum_{m \geq 0} \frac{\alpha^m \beta^{\binom{m}{2}}}{(1 + q)(1 + q + q^2) \cdots (1 + q + \cdots + q^{m-1})}.$$

Also, the *deformed exponential function* is

$$F(\alpha, \beta) = R(\alpha, \beta, 1) = \sum_{m \geq 0} \frac{\alpha^m \beta^{\binom{m}{2}}}{m!}. \tag{2.8.1}$$

Let $g(c, e, k)$ be the number of simple graphs with c connected components, e edges, and k vertices labeled $1, \ldots, k$ and $g'(e, k)$ be the number of simple *connected* graphs with e edges and k labeled vertices. Suppose that

$$G(t, y, z) = \sum_{c,e,k} g(c, e, k) t^c y^e \frac{z^k}{k!}$$

and

$$CG(y, z) = \sum_{e,k} g'(e, k) y^e \frac{z^k}{k!}.$$

Theorem 2.8.2. [11, 184] *The generating functions for counting simple graphs and simple connected graphs satisfy, respectively,*

$$G(t, y, z) = F(z, 1 + y)^t$$

and

$$CG(y, z) = \log F(z, 1 + y),$$

where F is the deformed exponential function (2.8.1).

2.9 DELETION CORRECTING CODES

A *Z-channel* (also called a *binary asymmetric channel*) is a channel with binary input and binary output where a transmitted 0 is always received correctly, but a transmitted 1 may be received as either 1 or 0. These channels have many applications, for example, some data storage systems and optical communication systems can be modelled using these channels. In 1965, Varshamov and Tenengolts [201] introduced an important class of codes, known as the *Varshamov–Tenengolts codes* or *VT codes*, that are capable of correcting asymmetric errors on a Z-channel (see also [200]).

Definition 2.9.1. Let n be a positive integer and $0 \le b \le n$ be a fixed integer. The *Varshamov–Tenengolts code* $VT_b(n)$ is the set of all binary vectors $\langle s_1, \ldots, s_n \rangle$ such that

$$\sum_{i=1}^{n} i s_i \equiv b \pmod{n + 1}.$$

In a *deletion channel*, n bits are transmitted but m bits ($m < n$) are received. Some bits are deleted, but neither sender nor the recipient knows which bits have been deleted and in which positions. Codes capable of correcting this type of error are called *deletion correcting codes*. These are a very important class of codes with many applications.

Now, we review some well-known classes of deletion correcting codes. Levenshtein [121] showed that VT codes are capable of correcting a single deletion. Despite the fact that the VT codes can correct only a single deletion, these codes and their variants have found many applications, including DNA-based data storage [67, 120] and distributed message synchronization [191, 203]. A generalization of VT codes to Abelian groups where the code length is one less than the order of the group was proposed by Constantin and Rao [45]; the size and weight distribution of the latter codes were studied by [55, 87, 102, 136].

Levenshtein [121] proved that any code that can correct s deletions (or s insertions) can also correct a total of s deletions and insertions. In the same paper, he also proposed the following important generalization of VT codes.

Definition 2.9.2. Let n, k be positive integers and $b \in \mathbb{Z}_n$. The *Levenshtein code* $L_b(k, n)$ is the set of all binary k-tuples $\langle s_1, \ldots, s_k \rangle$ such that

$$\sum_{i=1}^{k} i s_i \equiv b \pmod{n}.$$

By giving an elegant decoding algorithm, Levenshtein [121] showed that if $n \geq k + 1$, then the code $L_b(k, n)$ can correct a single deletion (and, consequently, can correct a single insertion). Furthermore, Levenshtein [121] proved that if $n \geq 2k$ then the code $L_b(k, n)$ can correct either a single deletion/insertion error or a single substitution error. The Levenshtein code has many interesting applications and is considered to be the most important deletion/insertion correcting code.

Motivated by applications in bursts of deletion correction, a variant of the Levenshtein code was introduced by [172] under the name of *Shifted Varshamov–Tenengolts codes*. Gabrys et al. [67] used Shifted VT codes to construct codes in the Damerau distance. Shifted VT codes combine a linear congruence constraint with a parity constraint, as stated in the next definition.

Definition 2.9.3. Let n, k be positive integers, $b \in \mathbb{Z}_n$, and $r \in \{0, 1\}$. The *Shifted Varshamov–Tenengolts code* $SVT_{b,r}(k, n)$ is the set of all binary k-tuples $\langle s_1, \ldots, s_k \rangle$ such that

$$\sum_{i=1}^{k} i s_i \equiv b \pmod{n}, \qquad \sum_{i=1}^{k} s_i \equiv r \pmod 2.$$

The reason why these codes are called 'shifted' is that they can correct a single deletion where the location of the deleted bit is known to be within certain consecutive positions. A variation of the Shifted VT codes has been presented by [48, 49].

Helberg and Ferreira [86] introduced a generalization of the Levenshtein code, referred to as the *Helberg code*, by replacing the coefficients (weights) i with modified versions of the Fibonacci numbers.

Definition 2.9.4. Let s, k be positive integers. The *Helberg code* $H_b(k, s)$ is the set of all binary k-tuples $\langle s_1, \ldots, s_k \rangle$ such that

$$\sum_{i=1}^{k} v_i s_i \equiv b \pmod{n},$$

where $v_i = 0$, for $i \le 0$; $v_i = 1 + \sum_{j=1}^{s} v_{i-j}$, for $i \ge 1$; $n = v_{k+1}$; and $b \in \mathbb{Z}_n$. Note that the multipliers v_i depend on s, and n depends on both s and k.

Clearly, the Helberg code with $s = 1$ coincides with the VT code. Helberg and Ferreira [86] gave numerical values for the maximum cardinality of this code for some special parameter choices. Abdel-Ghaar et al. [1] proved that the Helberg code can correct multiple deletion/insertion errors (see also [77] for a short proof of this result). Furthermore, multiple deletion correcting codes over non-binary alphabets generalizing the Helberg code were recently proposed by Le and Nguyen [115]. The Helberg code constraint was combined with the parity constraint of Shifted VT codes for the purpose of devising special types of DNA-based data storage codes by Gabrys et al. [67].

2.10 WEIGHT ENUMERATOR OF A CODE

The *Hamming weight* of a string over an alphabet is defined as the number of non-zero symbols in the string. For example, the Hamming weight of 01010 is 2, and the number of codewords in $VT_0(5)$ with Hamming weight 2 is 2.

The weight enumerator of a code is defined as follows.

Definition 2.10.1. Let k be a positive integer, $\mathbb{F}$ be a finite field, and $C \subseteq \mathbb{F}^k$. Then, the *weight enumerator* of the code C is defined as

$$W_C(z) = \sum_{\mathbf{c} \in C} z^{w(\mathbf{c})} = \sum_{t=0}^{k} N_t z^t,$$

where $w(\mathbf{c})$ is the Hamming weight of $\mathbf{c}$ and N_t is the number of codewords in C of Hamming weight t. Also, the *homogeneous weight enumerator* of the code C is defined as

$$W_C(x, y) = y^k W_C\left(\frac{x}{y}\right) = \sum_{t=0}^{k} N_t x^t y^{k-t}.$$

Clearly, by setting $z = 1$ in the weight enumerator (or $x = y = 1$ in the homogeneous weight enumerator), we obtain the size of code C, which we denote by $|C|$.

2.11 GAUSSIAN INTEGERS, SPECTRAL GRAPH THEORY, AND CHARACTERS

The ring of *Gaussian integers* is defined as

$$\mathbb{Z}[i] = \{x + yi : x, y \in \mathbb{Z}, i = \sqrt{-1}\}.$$

In other words, Gaussian integers are the lattice points in the Euclidean plane. The *norm* of a Gaussian integer $w = x + yi$ is $N(w) = |w|^2 = x^2 + y^2$. The elements of $\mathbb{Z}[i]$ with norm 1 are called the *units* of $\mathbb{Z}[i]$; so, the units of $\mathbb{Z}[i]$ are just ± 1 and $\pm i$.

Similarly, the ring of Gaussian integers modulo a positive integer n is defined as

$$\mathbb{Z}[i]/n\mathbb{Z}[i] \cong \mathbb{Z}_n[i] = \{a + bi : a, b \in \mathbb{Z}_n, i = \sqrt{-1}\}.$$

Note that the definition of norm (and so unit) in the ring $\mathbb{Z}_n[i]$ is the same as that of $\mathbb{Z}[i]$ except that we need to evaluate the norm modulo n. That is, the *norm* of $z = a + bi \in \mathbb{Z}_n[i]$ is $N(z) = a^2 + b^2 \pmod{n}$, and $z = a + bi \in \mathbb{Z}_n[i]$ is a *unit* of $\mathbb{Z}_n[i]$ if and only if

$$a^2 + b^2 \equiv 1 \pmod{n}.$$

The following classical result gives necessary and sufficient conditions under which the ring $\mathbb{Z}_n[i]$ is a field (see, e.g., [61, Fact 3]).

Proposition 2.11.1. *Let $n > 1$ be an integer. The ring $\mathbb{Z}_n[i]$ is a field if and only if n is a prime and $n \equiv 3 \pmod{4}$.*

Let Γ be a group written in additive notation. A non-empty subset $S \subseteq \Gamma$ is said to be *symmetric* if $S = -S$, where $-S = \{-x : x \in S\}$. In other words, S is symmetric if $-x \in S$ whenever $x \in S$. Now, we define Cayley graphs.

Definition 2.11.2. Let Γ be a group, written additively, and S be a finite symmetric subset of Γ that does not contain the identity element of Γ. The *Cayley graph* of Γ with respect to S, denoted by $G = \mathrm{Cay}(\Gamma, S)$, is the graph whose vertex set is Γ and such that $u \sim v$ if and only if $v - u \in S$. Note that the Cayley graph $G = \mathrm{Cay}(\Gamma, S)$ is undirected, simple, $|S|$-regular, and vertex-transitive. Also, G is connected if and only if S generates Γ.

Roughly speaking, an *expander* is a highly connected sparse graph, that is, every subset of its vertices has a large set of neighbors. An important special case, namely, Ramanujan graphs, are also of great interest. These graphs are actually 'optimal' expanders, from the spectral point of view. Roughly speaking, a *Ramanujan graph* is a connected regular graph whose second-largest eigenvalue in absolute value is 'asymptotically' the smallest possible (or, equivalently, whose spectral gap is 'asymptotically' the largest possible). Formally, a finite, connected, k-regular graph G is called a Ramanujan graph if every eigenvalue $\lambda \neq \pm k$ of G satisfies the bound

$$|\lambda| \leq 2\sqrt{k-1}.$$

To this date, there are only a few explicit constructions (which are useful for applications) of expanders and Ramanujan graphs, all given using several strong (and seemingly unrelated!) mathematical tools, mainly from number theory. These graphs have a great deal of seminal applications in many disciplines such as computer science, cryptography, coding theory, and even pure mathematics! See [51, 88, 129] for detailed discussions and surveys on expanders and Ramanujan graphs, their interactions with other areas like number theory and group theory, and their many wide-ranging applications.

Now, we review some basic facts about group characters (see, e.g., [94, 176] for more details). A *character* of a group Γ is a group homomorphism from Γ to the unit circle $S^1 = \{z \in \mathbb{C} : |z| = 1\}$. So, if Γ is a finite group, then a character of Γ can be defined as a group homomorphism from Γ to $\mathbb{C}^*$, the multiplicative group of non-zero complex numbers. For a group Γ, the *trivial* character χ_0 is the function on Γ where $\chi_0(g) = 1$, for all $g \in \Gamma$. The characters of a finite group are linearly independent. A finite group Γ has *at most* $|\Gamma|$ characters, and a finite Abelian group Γ has *exactly* $|\Gamma|$ distinct characters. For a finite Abelian group Γ with the trivial character χ_0,

$$\sum_{g \in \Gamma} \chi(g) = \begin{cases} |\Gamma|, & \text{if } \chi = \chi_0, \\ 0, & \text{if } \chi \neq \chi_0. \end{cases}$$

The following proposition lists some classical facts from spectral graph theory (see, e.g., [50]). As it is common, by an eigenvalue (resp., eigenvector) of a graph we mean an eigenvalue (resp., eigenvector) of the adjacency matrix of that graph.

Proposition 2.11.3. *Let G be a simple graph (i.e., without loops or multiple edges) of order n, with the adjacency matrix $A(G)$ and with the maximum degree $\Delta(G)$. Also, let $\lambda_{\min}(G)$ and $\lambda_{\max}(G)$ denote, respectively, the smallest and the largest eigenvalues of G. The following facts hold:*

- *The graph G has n eigenvalues (including multiplicities), and since $A(G)$ is real and symmetric, all these eigenvalues are real.*

- *We have $\lambda_{\max}(G) \leq \Delta(G)$. Furthermore, if G is k-regular, then $\lambda_{\max}(G) = k$, and for every eigenvalue λ of G, $|\lambda| \leq k$.*

- *If G is k-regular, then the multiplicity of the eigenvalue k equals the number of connected components of G. So, if G is k-regular, then G is connected if and only if the eigenvalue k has multiplicity one.*

- *The graph G is bipartite if and only if its spectrum is symmetric about 0. Also, if G is connected, then G is bipartite if and only if $\lambda_{\min}(G) = -\lambda_{\max}(G)$.*

It is well known that the spectra of Cayley graphs of finite groups can be expressed in terms of characters of the underlying group [13, 128]. The following result determines the eigenvalues and eigenvectors of Cayley graphs of finite Abelian groups. The theorem follows from a more general result of Lovász [128] (or of [13]).

Theorem 2.11.4. *Let Γ be a finite Abelian group, $\chi : \Gamma \to \mathbb{C}^*$ be a character of Γ, and S be a symmetric subset of Γ that does not contain the identity element of Γ. Then, the vector $v_\chi = (\chi(g))_{g \in \Gamma}$ is an eigenvector of the Cayley graph $G = \mathrm{Cay}(\Gamma, S)$, with the corresponding eigenvalue being*

$$\lambda_\chi = \sum_{s \in S} \chi(s).$$

CHAPTER 3

The GCD-Restricted Linear Congruences

3.1 INTRODUCTION

In this chapter, we study the number of solutions of the congruence (1.1.1) when the greatest common divisors (gcds) of coordinates x_i and the modulus n are certain numbers. More formally, we study the number of solutions when $(x_i, n) = t_i$ $(1 \le i \le k)$, where $t_1, \ldots, t_k$ are given positive divisors of n. To see how general the problem is, note that when all gcds are equal to 1 (that is, when $t_i = 1$), the problem is asking for the number of solutions of the congruence (1.1.1) when $x_i \in \mathbb{Z}_n^*$, where $\mathbb{Z}_n^*$ is the multiplicative group of integers modulo n.

The number of solutions of the congruence (1.1.1) when $x_i \in \mathbb{Z}_n^*$, which we call a *gcd-restricted linear congruence* or just *restricted linear congruence*, was investigated in special cases by several authors. It was shown by Rademacher [155] and Brauer [35] that the number $N_n(k, b)$ of solutions of the congruence $x_1 + \cdots +$

$x_k \equiv b \pmod{n}$ with the restrictions $(x_i, n) = 1 \ (1 \le i \le k)$ is

$$N_n(k, b) = \frac{\varphi(n)^k}{n} \prod_{p \mid n, p \mid b} \left(1 - \frac{(-1)^{k-1}}{(p-1)^{k-1}}\right) \prod_{p \mid n, p \nmid b} \left(1 - \frac{(-1)^k}{(p-1)^k}\right),$$

(3.1.1)

where $\varphi(n)$ is Euler's totient function and the products are taken over all prime divisors p of n. This result was rediscovered later by Dixon [58] and Rearick [159]. The equivalent formula

$$N_n(k, b) = \frac{1}{n} \sum_{d \mid n} c_d(b) \left(c_n\left(\frac{n}{d}\right)\right)^k,$$

(3.1.2)

involving the Ramanujan sums $c_n(m)$, was obtained by Nicol and Vandiver [150, Th. VII] and reproved by Cohen [42, Th. 6].

The special case of $k = 2$ was treated, independently, by Alder [6], Deaconescu [52], and Sander [166]. For $k = 2$ the function $N_n(2, b)$ coincides with Nagell's totient function (NAG) defined to be the number of integers $x \pmod{n}$ such that $(x, n) = (b - x, n) = 1$. From (3.1.1) one easily gets

$$N_n(2, b) = n \prod_{p \mid n, p \mid b} \left(1 - \frac{1}{p}\right) \prod_{p \mid n, p \nmid b} \left(1 - \frac{2}{p}\right).$$

(3.1.3)

From (3.1.3) it is clear that $N_n(2, 0) = \varphi(n)$ and

$$N_n(2, 1) = n \prod_{p \mid n} \left(1 - \frac{2}{p}\right).$$

(3.1.4)

Interestingly, the function $N_n(2, 1)$ was applied by D. N. Lehmer [117] in studying certain magic squares. It is also worth mentioning that the case of $k = 2$ is related to a long-standing conjecture due to D. H. Lehmer from 1932 (see [52, 53]) and also has interesting applications to Cayley graphs (see [166, 167]).

The problem in the case of k variables can be interpreted as a 'restricted partition problem modulo n' [150], or an equation in the ring $\mathbb{Z}_n$, where the solutions are its units [52, 166, 167]. More generally, it has connections to studying rings generated by their units, in particular in finding the number of representations of an element of a finite commutative ring, say R, as the sum of k units in R; see [101] and the references therein. The results of Ramanathan [156, Th. 5 and 6] are similar to (3.1.1) and (3.1.2), but in another context. See also McCarthy [135, Ch. 3] and Spilker [183] for further results with these and different restrictions on linear congruences.

The general case of the restricted linear congruence

$$a_1 x_1 + \cdots + a_k x_k \equiv b \pmod{n}, \quad (x_i, n) = t_i \ (1 \le i \le k),$$
$$(3.1.5)$$

was considered by Sburlati [168]. A formula for the number of solutions of (3.1.5) was deduced in Sburlati [168, Eq. 4 and 5] with some assumptions on the prime factors of n with respect to the values $a_i, t_i \ (1 \le i \le k)$ and with an incomplete proof. The special cases of $k = 2$ with $t_1 = t_2 = 1$ and $a_i = 1 \ (1 \le i \le k)$ of (3.1.5) were considered, respectively, by Sander and Sander [167] and Sun and Yang [189]. Cohen [44, Th. 4 and 5] derived two explicit formulas for the number of solutions of (3.1.5) with $t_i = 1, a_i \mid n, a_i$ prime $(1 \le i \le k)$. Jacobson and Williams [95] gave a nice explicit formula for the number of such solutions when $(a_1, \ldots, a_k) = t_i = 1 \ (1 \le i \le k)$. Also, the special case of $b = 0, a_i = 1, t_i = \frac{n}{m_i}, m_i \mid n \ (1 \le i \le k)$ is related to the *orbicyclic* (multivariate arithmetic) function [126], which has very interesting combinatorial and topological applications, in particular in counting non-isomorphic maps on orientable surfaces (see [21, 126, 137, 138, 193, 205]). The problem is also related to Harvey's famous theorem on the cyclic groups of automorphisms of compact Riemann surfaces; see Chapter 5. We also remark that, recently, Yang and Tang [211] considered the quadratic version of this problem in the special case of $k = 2, a_1 = a_2 = 1, t_1 = t_2 = 1$, and posed some problems for more general cases.

In the one-variable case, Alomair et al. [7], motivated by applications in designing an authenticated encryption scheme, gave a necessary and sufficient condition (with a long proof) for the congruence $ax \equiv b \pmod{n}$, with the restriction $(x, n) = 1$, to have a solution. Later, Grošek and Porubský [74] gave a short proof for this result, and also obtained a formula for the number of such solutions. In Theorem 3.2.1 (see Section 3.2) we deal with this problem in a more general form as a building block for the case of k variables $(k \geq 1)$.

In Section 3.2, we obtain an explicit formula for the number of solutions of the restricted linear congruence (3.1.5) for arbitrary integers $a_1, t_1, \ldots, a_k, t_k, b, n$ $(n \geq 1)$. Two major ingredients in the proofs are Ramanujan sums and the discrete Fourier transform (DFT) of arithmetic functions.

3.2 LINEAR CONGRUENCES WITH $(X_I, N) = T_I$ $(1 \leq I \leq K)$

In this section, using properties of Ramanujan sums and of the discrete Fourier transform of arithmetic functions, we derive an explicit formula for the number of solutions of the restricted linear congruence (3.1.5) for arbitrary integers $a_1, t_1, \ldots, a_k, t_k, b, n$ $(n \geq 1)$.

Let us start with the case that we have only one variable; this is a building block for the case of k variables $(k \geq 1)$. The following theorem generalizes the main result of [74], one of the main results of [7], and also a key lemma of [150, Lemma 1].

Theorem 3.2.1. *Let a, b, $n \geq 1$, and $t \geq 1$ be given integers. The congruence $ax \equiv b \pmod{n}$ has solution(s) x with $(x, n) = t$ if and only if $t \mid (b, n)$ and $\left(a, \frac{n}{t}\right) = \left(\frac{b}{t}, \frac{n}{t}\right)$. Furthermore, if these conditions are satisfied, then there are exactly*

$$\frac{\varphi\left(\frac{n}{t}\right)}{\varphi\left(\frac{n}{td}\right)} = d \prod_{\substack{p \mid d \\ p \nmid \frac{n}{td}}} \left(1 - \frac{1}{p}\right) \tag{3.2.1}$$

solutions, where p ranges over the primes and $d = \left(a, \frac{n}{t}\right) = \left(\frac{b}{t}, \frac{n}{t}\right)$.

Proof. Assume that there is a solution x satisfying $ax \equiv b$ (mod n) and $(x, n) = t$. Then, $(ax, n) = (b, n) = td$, for some d. Thus, $t \mid (b, n)$ and $\left(\frac{ax}{t}, \frac{n}{t}\right) = \left(\frac{b}{t}, \frac{n}{t}\right) = d$. But, since $\left(\frac{x}{t}, \frac{n}{t}\right) = 1$, we have $\left(a, \frac{n}{t}\right) = \left(\frac{b}{t}, \frac{n}{t}\right) = d$.

Now, let $t \mid (b, n)$ and $\left(a, \frac{n}{t}\right) = \left(\frac{b}{t}, \frac{n}{t}\right) = d$. Let us denote $A = \frac{a}{d}$, $B = \frac{b}{dt}$, and $N = \frac{n}{dt}$. Then, $(A, N) = (B, N) = 1$. Since $(A, N) = 1$, the congruence $Ay \equiv B$ (mod N) has a unique solution $y_0 = A^{-1}B$ (mod N) and $(Ay_0, N) = (B, N)$, that is, $(y_0, N) = 1$. It follows that $a(ty_0) \equiv b$ (mod n), which shows that $x_0 = ty_0$ is a solution of $ax \equiv b$ (mod n).

If x is such that $ax \equiv b$ (mod n) and $(x, n) = t$, then $x = ty$ and $Ay \equiv B$ (mod N). Hence, all solutions of the congruence $ax \equiv b$ (mod n) with $(x, n) = t$ have the form $x = t(y_0 + kN)$, where $0 \leq k \leq d - 1$ and $\left(y_0 + kN, \frac{n}{t}\right) = 1$. Since $(y_0, N) = 1$, the latter condition is equivalent to $(y_0 + kN, d) = 1$. The number S of such solutions, using the characteristic property (2.1.9) of the Möbius function, is

$$
S = \sum_{\substack{0 \leq k \leq d-1 \\ (y_0+kN, d)=1}} 1
$$

$$
= \sum_{0 \leq k \leq d-1} \sum_{\delta \mid (y_0+kN, d)} \mu(\delta)
$$

$$
= \sum_{\delta \mid d} \mu(\delta) \sum_{\substack{0 \leq k \leq d-1 \\ \delta \mid y_0+kN}} 1 = \sum_{\delta \mid d} \mu(\delta) \sum_{\substack{0 \leq k \leq d-1 \\ kN \equiv -y_0 \ (\text{mod } \delta)}} 1.
$$

Here, if $v = (N, \delta) > 1$, then $v \nmid y_0$ since $(y_0, N) = 1$. Thus, the congruence $kN \equiv -y_0$ (mod δ) has no solution in k and the inner sum is zero. If $(N, \delta) = 1$, then the same congruence has one solution in k (mod δ) and has $\frac{d}{\delta}$ (mod d) solutions. Therefore,

$$S = \sum_{\substack{\delta \mid d \\ (\delta, N) = 1}} \mu(\delta) \frac{d}{\delta} = d \prod_{\substack{p \mid d \\ p \nmid N}} \left(1 - \frac{1}{p}\right) = \frac{\varphi(Nd)}{\varphi(N)} = \frac{\varphi\left(\frac{n}{t}\right)}{\varphi\left(\frac{n}{td}\right)}.$$

The proof is now complete. ☐

Remark 3.2.2. [7] *only proved the first part of Theorem 3.2.1 in the case of $t = 1$, and applied the result in checking the integrity of their authenticated encryption scheme. Their main result [7, Th. 5.11] is obtained via a very long argument; however, formula (3.2.1) alone gives a one-line proof for their theorem that we omit here.*

Corollary 3.2.3. *The congruence $ax \equiv b$ (mod n) has exactly one solution x with $(x, n) = t$ if and only if one of the following two cases holds:*

(i) $\left(a, \frac{n}{t}\right) = \left(\frac{b}{t}, \frac{n}{t}\right) = 1$, where $t \mid (b, n)$;

(ii) $\left(a, \frac{n}{t}\right) = \left(\frac{b}{t}, \frac{n}{t}\right) = 2$, where $t \mid b$, $n = 2^r u$, $r \geq 1$, $u \geq 1$ is odd, $t = 2^{r-1} v$, and $v \mid u$.

Proof. Let $d = \left(a, \frac{n}{t}\right) = \left(\frac{b}{t}, \frac{n}{t}\right)$. If $d = 1$, then (3.2.1) shows that there is one solution. Now, for $d > 1$ it is enough to consider the case when $d = p^j$ ($j \geq 1$) is a prime power. Let $p^r \parallel n$, $p^s \parallel t$ with $0 \leq j + s \leq r$. Then, by (3.2.1), there is one solution if $p^j(1 - \frac{1}{p}) = 1$ provided that $p \nmid p^{r-s-j}$. This holds only in the case $p = 2, j = 1$, $s + j = r$. This gives $d = 2$ together with the conditions formulated in (ii). ☐

We remark that Corollary 3.2.3, in the case of $t = 1$, was obtained by Grošek and Porubský [74, Cor. 4].

Now, we deal with the case of k variables ($k \geq 1$). Assume that $a_1, \ldots, a_k, b$ are fixed, and let $N_n(t_1, \ldots, t_k)$ denote the number of incongruent solutions of (3.1.5). We note the following multiplicative property: If $n, m \geq 1$ and $(n, m) = 1$, then

$$N_{nm}(t_1, \ldots, t_k) = N_n(u_1, \ldots, u_k)N_m(v_1, \ldots, v_k), \qquad (3.2.2)$$

with unique u_i, v_i such that $t_i = u_i v_i, u_i \mid n, v_i \mid m \, (1 \leq i \leq k)$. This can be easily shown by the Chinese remainder theorem. Therefore, it would be enough to obtain $N_n(t_1, \ldots, t_k)$ in the case $n = p^r$, a prime power. However, we prefer to derive the next compact results, which are valid for an arbitrary positive integer n.

In the case that $a_i = 1 \, (1 \leq i \leq k)$, we prove the following result.

Theorem 3.2.4. *Let $b, n \geq 1, t_i \mid n \, (1 \leq i \leq k)$ be given integers. The number of solutions of the linear congruence $x_1 + \cdots + x_k \equiv b \pmod{n}$, with $(x_i, n) = t_i \, (1 \leq i \leq k)$, is*

$$N_n(b; t_1, \ldots, t_k) = \frac{1}{n}\sum_{d \mid n} c_d(b) \prod_{i=1}^{k} c_{\frac{n}{t_i}}\left(\frac{n}{d}\right) \geq 0. \qquad (3.2.3)$$

Proof. Apply the properties of the DFT. Observe that

$$(\varrho_{n,t_1} \otimes \cdots \otimes \varrho_{n,t_k})(b) = \sum_{\substack{1 \leq x_1, \ldots, x_k \leq n \\ x_1 + \ldots + x_k \equiv b \pmod{n} \\ (x_i, n) = t_i, \, 1 \leq i \leq k}} 1$$

is exactly the number $N_n(b; t_1, \ldots, t_k)$ of solutions of the given restricted congruence.

Therefore, by (2.3.3) and Theorem 2.3.1,

$$\widehat{N_n}(b; t_1, \ldots, t_k) = c_{\frac{n}{t_1}}(b) \cdots c_{\frac{n}{t_k}}(b),$$

where the variable for the DFT is b ($n, t_1, \ldots, t_k$ being parameters). Now, the IDFT formula (2.3.2) gives

$$N_n(b; t_1, \ldots, t_k) = \frac{1}{n} \sum_{j=1}^{n} c_{\frac{n}{t_1}}(j) \cdots c_{\frac{n}{t_k}}(j) e\left(\frac{bj}{n}\right).$$

By Corollary 2.1.4(iii) and the associativity of gcd, one has for every i ($1 \le i \le k$),

$$c_{\frac{n}{t_i}}((j, n)) = c_{\frac{n}{t_i}}\left(\left((j, n), \frac{n}{t_i}\right)\right) = c_{\frac{n}{t_i}}\left(\left(j, \left(n, \frac{n}{t_i}\right)\right)\right)$$

$$= c_{\frac{n}{t_i}}\left(\left(j, \frac{n}{t_i}\right)\right) = c_{\frac{n}{t_i}}(j).$$

$$(3.2.4)$$

The properties (3.2.4) show that $m \mapsto c_{\frac{n}{t_1}}(m) \cdots c_{\frac{n}{t_k}}(m)$ is an n-even function. Now, by applying Theorem 2.3.2, we obtain (3.2.3). □

Remark 3.2.5. *Note that a slight modification of the proof of Tóth [193, Prop. 21] furnishes an alternate proof for Theorem 3.2.4. Sun and Yang [189] obtained a different formula (with a longer proof) for the number of solutions of the linear congruence in Theorem 3.2.4, but we need the equivalent formula (3.2.3) for the purposes of this chapter (see also [23] for another equivalent formula). We also remark that the special case of $b = 0$, $t_i = \frac{n}{m_i}$, $m_i \mid n$ ($1 \le i \le k$) gives the function*

$$E(m_1, \ldots, m_k) = \frac{1}{n} \sum_{d \mid n} \varphi(d) \prod_{i=1}^{k} c_{m_i}\left(\frac{n}{d}\right),$$

which was shown by Tóth [193, Prop. 9] to be equivalent to the orbicyclic (multivariate arithmetic) function defined by

Liskovets [126] as

$$E(m_1, \ldots, m_k) := \frac{1}{n} \sum_{q=1}^{n} \prod_{i=1}^{k} c_{m_i}(q).$$

The orbicyclic function, $E(m_1, \ldots, m_k)$, has very interesting combinatorial and topological applications, in particular, in counting non-isomorphic maps on orientable surfaces, and was investigated by [21], [126], [137], [193], [138], and [205].

Now, using Theorem 3.2.1 and Theorem 3.2.4, we obtain the following general formula for the number of solutions of the restricted linear congruence (3.1.5).

Theorem 3.2.6. *Let $a_i, t_i, b, n \in \mathbb{Z}$, $n \geq 1$, and $t_i \mid n$ ($1 \leq i \leq k$). The number of solutions of the linear congruence $a_1 x_1 + \cdots + a_k x_k \equiv b \pmod{n}$, with $(x_i, n) = t_i$ ($1 \leq i \leq k$), is*

$$N_n(b; a_1, t_1, \ldots, a_k, t_k)$$

$$= \frac{1}{n} \left(\prod_{i=1}^{k} \frac{\varphi\left(\frac{n}{t_i}\right)}{\varphi\left(\frac{n}{t_i d_i}\right)} \right) \sum_{d \mid n} c_d(b) \prod_{i=1}^{k} c_{\frac{n}{t_i d_i}}\left(\frac{n}{d}\right) \qquad (3.2.5)$$

$$= \frac{1}{n} \left(\prod_{i=1}^{k} \varphi\left(\frac{n}{t_i}\right) \right) \sum_{d \mid n} c_d(b) \prod_{i=1}^{k} \frac{\mu\left(\frac{d}{(a_i t_i, d)}\right)}{\varphi\left(\frac{d}{(a_i t_i, d)}\right)}, \qquad (3.2.6)$$

where $d_i = (a_i, \frac{n}{t_i})$ ($1 \leq i \leq k$).

Proof. Assume that the linear congruence $a_1 x_1 + \cdots + a_k x_k \equiv b$ (mod n) has a solution $\langle x_1, \ldots, x_k \rangle \in \mathbb{Z}_n^k$ with $(x_i, n) = t_i$ ($1 \leq i \leq k$). Let $a_i x_i \equiv y_i \pmod{n}$ ($1 \leq i \leq k$). Then, $(a_i x_i, n) = (y_i, n) = t_i d_i$, for some d_i ($1 \leq i \leq k$). Thus, $(\frac{a_i x_i}{t_i}, \frac{n}{t_i}) = (\frac{y_i}{t_i}, \frac{n}{t_i}) = d_i$. But, since $(\frac{x_i}{t_i}, \frac{n}{t_i}) = 1$, we have $d_i = (a_i, \frac{n}{t_i}) = (\frac{y_i}{t_i}, \frac{n}{t_i})$.

By Theorem 3.2.4, the number of solutions of the linear congruence $y_1 + \cdots + y_k \equiv b \pmod{n}$, with $(y_i, n) = t_i d_i$ $(1 \leq i \leq k)$, is

$$\frac{1}{n} \sum_{d \mid n} c_d(b) \prod_{i=1}^{k} c_{\frac{n}{t_i d_i}} \left(\frac{n}{d} \right). \qquad (3.2.7)$$

Now, given the solutions $\langle y_1, \ldots, y_k \rangle$ of the latter congruence, we need to find the number of solutions of $a_i x_i \equiv y_i \pmod{n}$, with $(x_i, n) = t_i$ $(1 \leq i \leq k)$. Since $(a_i, \frac{n}{t_i}) = (\frac{y_i}{t_i}, \frac{n}{t_i}) = d_i$, by Theorem 3.2.1, the latter congruence has exactly

$$\frac{\varphi(\frac{n}{t_i})}{\varphi(\frac{n}{t_i d_i})} \qquad (3.2.8)$$

solutions. Combining (3.2.7) and (3.2.8), we get the formula (3.2.5).

Furthermore, applying von Sterneck's formula (2.1.12), we deduce

$$c_{\frac{n}{t_i d_i}} \left(\frac{n}{d} \right) = \frac{\varphi(\frac{n}{t_i d_i}) \mu(w_i)}{\varphi(w_i)}, \qquad (3.2.9)$$

where, denoting by $[a, b]$ the least common multiple (lcm) of the integers a and b,

$$w_i = \frac{\frac{n}{t_i d_i}}{(\frac{n}{t_i d_i}, \frac{n}{d})} = \frac{\frac{n}{t_i d_i}}{\frac{n}{[t_i d_i, d]}} = \frac{[t_i d_i, d]}{t_i d_i} = \frac{d}{(t_i d_i, d)}$$

$$= \frac{d}{((a_i t_i, n), d)} = \frac{d}{(a_i t_i, d)}.$$

By inserting (3.2.9) into (3.2.5) we get (3.2.6). $\qquad \square$

Remark 3.2.7. *For fixed a_i, t_i $(1 \leq i \leq k)$ and fixed n, the function*

$$b \mapsto N_n(b; a_1, t_1, \ldots, a_k, t_k)$$

is an even function (mod *n*). *This follows from* (3.2.5), *showing that*

$$N_n(b; a_1, t_1, \ldots, a_k, t_k)$$

is a linear combination of the functions $b \mapsto c_d(b)$ $(d \mid n)$, *which are all even* (mod *n*) *by* (2.1.5) *and* (3.2.4).

Remark 3.2.8. *In the case of* $k = 1$, *by comparing Theorem 3.2.1 with* (3.2.5) *and by denoting* $t_1 d_1 = s$, *we obtain, as a byproduct, the following identity, which is similar to* (2.1.13) *(and can also be proved directly): If* $b, n \in \mathbb{Z}$, $n \geq 1$, *and* $s \mid n$, *then*

$$\sum_{d \mid n} c_d(b) c_{\frac{n}{s}}\left(\frac{n}{d}\right) = \begin{cases} n, & \text{if } (b, n) = s, \\ 0, & \text{if } (b, n) \neq s. \end{cases} \tag{3.2.10}$$

Though Theorem 3.2.6 is useful from several aspects (e.g., we use it in the proof of Theorem 5.2.1), for many applications we need a more explicit formula.

If in (3.1.5) one has $a_i = 0$ for every $1 \leq i \leq k$, then clearly there are solutions $\langle x_1, \ldots, x_k \rangle$ if and only if $b \equiv 0$ (mod *n*) and $t_i \mid n$ $(1 \leq i \leq k)$, and in this case there are $\varphi(\frac{n}{t_1}) \cdots \varphi(\frac{n}{t_k})$ solutions.

Consider the restricted linear congruence (3.1.5) and assume that there is an i_0 such that $a_{i_0} \neq 0$. For every prime divisor p of n, let r_p be the exponent of p in the prime factorization of n, and let $m_p = m_p(a_1, t_1, \ldots, a_k, t_k)$ denote the smallest $j \geq 1$ such that there is some i with $p^j \nmid a_i t_i$. There exists a finite m_p for every p, since for a sufficiently large j one has $p^j \nmid a_{i_0} t_{i_0}$. Furthermore, let

$$e_p = e_p(a_1, t_1, \ldots, a_k, t_k) = \#\{i : 1 \leq i \leq k, p^{m_p} \nmid a_i t_i\}.$$

By definition, $1 \leq e_p \leq$ the number of i such that $a_i \neq 0$. Note that in many situations instead of $m_p(a_1, t_1, \ldots, a_k, t_k)$ we write m_p, and instead of $e_p(a_1, t_1, \ldots, a_k, t_k)$ we write e_p for short. However, it is important to note that both m_p and e_p always depend on $a_1, t_1, \ldots, a_k, t_k, p$.

Theorem 3.2.9. *Let $a_i, t_i, b, n \in \mathbb{Z}$, $n \geq 1$, $t_i \mid n$ $(1 \leq i \leq k)$ and assume that $a_i \neq 0$ for at least one i. Consider the linear congruence $a_1 x_1 + \cdots + a_k x_k \equiv b \pmod{n}$, with $(x_i, n) = t_i$ $(1 \leq i \leq k)$. If there is a prime $p \mid n$ such that $m_p \leq r_p$ and $p^{m_p-1} \nmid b$ or $m_p \geq r_p + 1$ and $p^{r_p} \nmid b$, then the linear congruence has no solution. Otherwise, the number of solutions is*

$$\prod_{i=1}^{k} \varphi\left(\frac{n}{t_i}\right) \prod_{\substack{p \mid n \\ m_p \leq r_p \\ p^{m_p} \mid b}} p^{m_p - r_p - 1}\left(1 - \frac{(-1)^{e_p - 1}}{(p-1)^{e_p - 1}}\right)$$

$$\prod_{\substack{p \mid n \\ m_p \leq r_p \\ p^{m_p - 1} \| b}} p^{m_p - r_p - 1}\left(1 - \frac{(-1)^{e_p}}{(p-1)^{e_p}}\right), \qquad (3.2.11)$$

where the last two products are over the prime factors p of n with the given additional properties. Note that the last product is empty and equal to 1 if $b = 0$.

Proof. For a prime power $n = p^{r_p}$ $(r_p \geq 1)$, the inner sum of (3.2.6) is

$$W := \sum_{d \mid p^{r_p}} c_d(b) \prod_{i=1}^{k} \frac{\mu\left(\frac{d}{(a_i t_i, d)}\right)}{\varphi\left(\frac{d}{(a_i t_i, d)}\right)} = \sum_{j=0}^{r_p} c_{p^j}(b) \prod_{i=1}^{k} \frac{\mu\left(\frac{p^j}{(a_i t_i, p^j)}\right)}{\varphi\left(\frac{p^j}{(a_i t_i, p^j)}\right)}.$$

Assume that $m_p \leq r_p$. Then, $p^{m_p-1} \mid a_i t_i$ for every i and $p^{m_p} \nmid a_i t_i$ for at least one i. Therefore, $(a_i t_i, p^j) = p^j$ if $0 \leq j \leq m_p - 1$. Also, $(a_i t_i, p^{m_p}) = p^{m_p-1}$ if $p^{m_p} \nmid a_i t_i$, and this holds for e_p distinct values of i. We obtain

$$W = \sum_{j=0}^{m_p-1} c_{p^j}(b) + c_{p^{m_p}}(b)\frac{(-1)^{e_p}}{(p-1)^{e_p}},$$

where the other terms are zero. We deduce by using (2.1.8) and (2.1.10) that

$$W = \begin{cases} p^{m_p-1}\left(1 - \frac{(-1)^{e_p-1}}{(p-1)^{e_p-1}}\right), & \text{if } p^{m_p} \mid b, \\ p^{m_p-1}\left(1 - \frac{(-1)^{e_p}}{(p-1)^{e_p}}\right), & \text{if } p^{m_p-1} \parallel b, \\ 0, & \text{if } p^{m_p-1} \nmid b. \end{cases} \qquad (3.2.12)$$

Now, assume that $m_p \geq r_p + 1$. Then, $p^{r_p} \mid a_i t_i$ for every i and $(a_i t_i, p^j) = p^j$ for every j with $0 \leq j \leq r_p$. Hence, by using (2.1.8),

$$W = \sum_{j=1}^{r_p} c_{p^j}(b) = \begin{cases} p^{r_p}, & \text{if } p^{r_p} \mid b, \\ 0, & \text{if } p^{r_p} \nmid b. \end{cases}$$

Inserting into (3.2.6) and by using the multiplicative property (3.2.2), we deduce that there is no solution in the specified cases. Otherwise, the number of solutions is given by

$$\prod_{p \mid n} p^{-r_p} \prod_{i=1}^{k} \varphi\left(\frac{n}{t_i}\right) \prod_{\substack{p \mid n \\ m_p \geq r_p+1 \\ p^{r_p} \mid b}} p^{r_p} \prod_{\substack{p \mid n \\ m_p \leq r_p \\ p^{m_p} \mid b}} p^{m_p-1}\left(1 - \frac{(-1)^{e_p-1}}{(p-1)^{e_p-1}}\right)$$

$$\times \prod_{\substack{p \mid n \\ m_p \leq r_p \\ p^{m_p-1} \parallel b}} p^{m_p-r_p-1}\left(1 - \frac{(-1)^{e_p}}{(p-1)^{e_p}}\right),$$

where the multiplicative property is also applied to the product of the φ factors. This gives (3.2.11). $\qquad \square$

Interestingly, if in Theorem 3.2.9 we put $a_i = t_i = 1$ $(1 \leq i \leq k)$, then we get the following result first proved by Rademacher [155] and Brauer [35].

Corollary 3.2.10. *Let $b, n \in \mathbb{Z}$ and $n \geq 1$. The number of solutions of the linear congruence $x_1 + \cdots + x_k \equiv b$ (mod n), with $(x_i, n) = 1$ $(1 \leq i \leq k)$, is*

$$\frac{\varphi(n)^k}{n} \prod_{p \mid n, p \mid b} \left(1 - \frac{(-1)^{k-1}}{(p-1)^{k-1}}\right) \prod_{p \mid n, p \nmid b} \left(1 - \frac{(-1)^k}{(p-1)^k}\right).$$

Proof. Since $a_i = t_i = 1$ $(1 \leq i \leq k)$, for every prime divisor p of n, we have $m_p = 1$ and $e_p = k$. So, for every prime divisor p of n, we also have $m_p = 1 \leq r_p$. Clearly, the first part of Theorem 3.2.9 does not hold in this special case, that is, there is no prime $p \mid n$ such that $m_p \leq r_p$ and $p^{m_p - 1} \nmid b$ or $m_p \geq r_p + 1$ and $p^{r_p} \nmid b$. Furthermore, we have

$$\prod_{p \mid n, p \mid b} p^{r_p} \prod_{p \mid n, p \nmid b} p^{r_p} = n.$$

Thus, the result follows by a simple application of the second part of Theorem 3.2.9 (3.2.11). □

Corollary 3.2.11. *The restricted congruence given in Theorem 3.2.9 has no solutions if and only if one of the following cases holds:*

(i) *there is a prime $p \mid n$ with $m_p \leq r_p$ and $p^{m_p - 1} \nmid b$;*

(ii) *there is a prime $p \mid n$ with $m_p \geq r_p + 1$ and $p^{r_p} \nmid b$;*

(iii) *there is a prime $p \mid n$ with $m_p \leq r_p$, $e_p = 1$ and $p^{m_p} \mid b$;*

(iv) *n is even, $m_2 \leq r_2$, e_2 is odd, and $2^{m_2} \mid b$;*

(v) *n is even, $m_2 \leq r_2$, e_2 is even, and $2^{m_2 - 1} \| b$.*

Proof. Use the first part of Theorem 3.2.9, and examine the conditions under which the factors of the products in (3.2.11) vanish. □

We note that, though Theorem 3.2.9 may seem a bit complicated, it is in fact easy to work with. Here, we show, via several examples, how to apply Theorem 3.2.9.

Example 3.2.12:

(i) Consider $2x_1 + x_2 + 2x_3 \equiv 12 \pmod{24}$, with $(x_1, 24) = 3$, $(x_2, 24) = 2$, and $(x_3, 24) = 4$.

Here, $24 = 2^3 \cdot 3$; $2 \mid a_1 t_1 = 6$, $2 \mid a_2 t_2 = 2$, $2 \mid a_3 t_3 = 8$; $2^2 \nmid a_1 t_1 = 6$, $2^2 \nmid a_2 t_2 = 2$, $2^2 \mid a_3 t_3 = 8$, hence $e_2 = 2$ and $m_2 = 2$, also $2^2 \mid b = 12$; $3 \mid a_1 t_1 = 6$, $3 \nmid a_2 t_2 = 2$, $3 \nmid a_3 t_3 = 8$, hence $e_3 = 2$, $m_3 = 1$, also $3^1 \mid b = 12$.

The number of solutions is

$$N = \varphi(24/3)\varphi(24/2)\varphi(24/4)2^{2-3-1}$$

$$\left(1 - \frac{(-1)^{2-1}}{(2-1)^{2-1}}\right) 3^{1-1-1} \left(1 - \frac{(-1)^{2-1}}{(3-1)^{2-1}}\right) = 8.$$

(ii) Now, let $2x_1 + x_2 + 2x_3 \equiv 4 \pmod{24}$, with $(x_1, 24) = 3$, $(x_2, 24) = 2$, and $(x_3, 24) = 4$, where only b is changed.

Here, $2^2 \mid b = 4$, $3^{1-1} \parallel b = 4$.

The number of solutions is

$$N = \varphi(24/3)\varphi(24/2)\varphi(24/4)2^{2-3-1}$$

$$\left(1 - \frac{(-1)^{2-1}}{(2-1)^{2-1}}\right) 3^{1-1-1} \left(1 - \frac{(-1)^2}{(3-1)^2}\right) = 4.$$

(iii) Let $2x_1 + x_2 + 2x_3 \equiv 5 \pmod{24}$, with $(x_1, 24) = 3$, $(x_2, 24) = 2$, and $(x_3, 24) = 4$, where again only b is changed.

Here, $2^{2-1} \nmid b = 5$, hence there are no solutions by Corollary 3.2.11(i). (Well, this is obvious, since all terms have to be even, but 5 is odd.)

(iv) Let $2x_1 + x_2 + 2x_3 \equiv 10 \pmod{24}$, with $(x_1, 24) = 3$, $(x_2, 24) = 2$, and $(x_3, 24) = 4$, where again only b is changed.

Here, $2^{2-1} \parallel b = 10$, hence there is no solution by Corollary 3.2.11(v).

Corollary 3.2.11 is the only result in the literature that gives *necessary and sufficient conditions* for the (non-)existence of solutions of restricted linear congruences in their most general case. We believe that Theorem 3.2.9 and Corollary 3.2.11 are strong tools that may lead to interesting applications/implications (see Chapters 4, 5, and 9).

Remark 3.2.13. *If $k = 1$ then $e_p = 1$ for every prime $p \mid n$, and it is easy to see that from Theorem 3.2.9 and Corollary 3.2.11, we reobtain Theorem 3.2.1.*

The following formula is a special case of Theorem 3.2.9 and was obtained by Sburlati [168] with an incomplete proof.

Corollary 3.2.14. *Assume that for every prime $p \mid n$ one has $m_p = 1$, that is, $p \nmid a_i t_i$ for at least one $i \in \{1, \ldots, k\}$. Then, the number of solutions of the restricted linear congruence (3.1.5) is*

$$\frac{1}{n} \prod_{i=1}^{k} \varphi\left(\frac{n}{t_i}\right) \prod_{p \mid n, p \mid b} \left(1 - \frac{(-1)^{e_p - 1}}{(p-1)^{e_p - 1}}\right) \prod_{p \mid n, p \nmid b} \left(1 - \frac{(-1)^{e_p}}{(p-1)^{e_p}}\right).$$

$$(3.2.13)$$

3.3 AN EQUIVALENT FORM OF THEOREM 3.2.4

Now, we combine ideas from the finite Fourier transform of arithmetic functions and Ramanujan sums to present a new and short proof for an equivalent form of Theorem 3.2.4 with the hope that its idea might be applicable to other relevant problems. In fact, as problems of this kind have many applications, having generalizations and/or new proofs and/or equivalent formulas for this problem may lead to further work. This theorem generalizes the main results of [42], [58], [150], and [167] and one of the main results of [166], and also gives an equivalent formula for the main result of [189].

Theorem 3.3.1. *Let $b, n \in \mathbb{Z}$, $n \geq 1$, and $\mathcal{D}_1, \ldots, \mathcal{D}_{\tau(n)}$ be all positive divisors of n. For $1 \leq l \leq \tau(n)$, define $C_l := \{1 \leqslant x \leqslant n : (x, n) = \mathcal{D}_l\}$. The number of solutions of the linear congruence $x_1 + \cdots + x_k \equiv b \pmod{n}$, with $\kappa_l = |\{x_1, \ldots, x_k\} \cap C_l|$, $1 \leq l \leq \tau(n)$, is*

$$\frac{1}{n} \sum_{d \mid n} c_d(b) \prod_{l=1}^{\tau(n)} \left(c_{\frac{n}{\mathcal{D}_l}}(d) \right)^{\kappa_l}. \tag{3.3.1}$$

Proof. Suppose that $\widehat{f_n}(k, b)$ denotes the number of solutions of the linear congruence $x_1 + \cdots + x_k \equiv b \pmod{n}$, with $\kappa_l = |\{x_1, \ldots, x_k\} \cap C_l|$, $1 \leq l \leq \tau(n)$. One can observe that, for every $m \in \mathbb{N}$, we have

$$\sum_{b=1}^{n} \widehat{f_n}(k, b) e\left(\frac{bm}{n} \right) = \prod_{l=1}^{\tau(n)} \left(\sum_{x \in C_l} e\left(\frac{mx}{n} \right) \right)^{\kappa_l}. \tag{3.3.2}$$

First, we give a short combinatorial argument to justify (3.3.2). Here, the key idea is that $\widehat{f_n}(k, b)$ can be interpreted as the number of possible ways of writing b as a sum modulo n of κ_1 elements of C_1, κ_2 elements of C_2, $\ldots$, $\kappa_{\tau(n)}$ elements of $C_{\tau(n)}$. Now, expand the right-hand side of (3.3.2). Note that each term of this expansion has $e(\frac{m}{n})$ as a factor (compare this to the left-hand side of (3.3.2)). Also, note that the exponent of each term of this expansion (ignoring m) is just a sum of some elements of $C_1, \ldots, C_{\tau(n)}$, which equals b ($1 \leq b \leq n$). In fact, recalling our interpretation of $\widehat{f_n}(k, b)$, we can see that in this expansion there are exactly $\widehat{f_n}(k, 1)$ terms of the form $e(\frac{m}{n})$, $\widehat{f_n}(k, 2)$ terms of the form $e(\frac{2m}{n})$, $\ldots$,

$\widehat{f}_n(k, n)$ terms of the form $e(m)$; that is, there are exactly $\widehat{f}_n(k, b)$ terms of the form $e(\frac{bm}{n})$, for $1 \le b \le n$. Therefore, we get the left-hand side of (3.3.2).

Putting $x'_l = \frac{x}{\mathcal{D}_l}$, $1 \le l \le \tau(n)$, we get

$$\sum_{x \in \mathcal{C}_l} e\left(\frac{mx}{n}\right) = \sum_{\substack{x=1 \\ (x,n)=\mathcal{D}_l}}^{n} e\left(\frac{mx}{n}\right) = \sum_{\substack{x'_l=1 \\ (x'_l, n/\mathcal{D}_l)=1}}^{n/\mathcal{D}_l} e\left(\frac{mx'_l}{n/\mathcal{D}_l}\right) = c_{\frac{n}{\mathcal{D}_l}}(m).$$

Therefore,

$$\sum_{b=1}^{n} \widehat{f}_n(k, b) e\left(\frac{bm}{n}\right) = \prod_{l=1}^{\tau(n)} \left(c_{\frac{n}{\mathcal{D}_l}}(m)\right)^{\kappa_l}.$$

Now, by (2.3.1) and (2.3.2), and since $c_{\frac{n}{\mathcal{D}_l}}(m) = c_{\frac{n}{\mathcal{D}_l}}((m,n))$, we have

$$\widehat{f}_n(k, b) = \frac{1}{n} \sum_{m=1}^{n} e\left(\frac{-bm}{n}\right) \prod_{l=1}^{\tau(n)} \left(c_{\frac{n}{\mathcal{D}_l}}(m)\right)^{\kappa_l}$$

$$= \frac{1}{n} \sum_{d \mid n} \sum_{\substack{m=1 \\ (m,n)=d}}^{n} e\left(\frac{-bm}{n}\right) \prod_{l=1}^{\tau(n)} \left(c_{\frac{n}{\mathcal{D}_l}}(m)\right)^{\kappa_l}$$

$$= \frac{1}{n} \sum_{d \mid n} \sum_{\substack{m=1 \\ (m,n)=d}}^{n} e\left(\frac{-bm}{n}\right) \prod_{l=1}^{\tau(n)} \left(c_{\frac{n}{\mathcal{D}_l}}(d)\right)^{\kappa_l}$$

$$\overset{m'=m/d}{=} \frac{1}{n} \sum_{d \mid n} \sum_{\substack{m'=1 \\ (m',n/d)=1}}^{n/d} e\left(\frac{-bm'}{n/d}\right) \prod_{l=1}^{\tau(n)} \left(c_{\frac{n}{\mathcal{D}_l}}(d)\right)^{\kappa_l}$$

$$= \frac{1}{n} \sum_{d \mid n} c_{n/d}(-b) \prod_{l=1}^{\tau(n)} \left(c_{\frac{n}{\mathcal{D}_l}}(d) \right)^{\kappa_l}$$

$$= \frac{1}{n} \sum_{d \mid n} c_{n/d}(b) \prod_{l=1}^{\tau(n)} \left(c_{\frac{n}{\mathcal{D}_l}}(d) \right)^{\kappa_l}$$

$$= \frac{1}{n} \sum_{d \mid n} c_d(b) \prod_{l=1}^{\tau(n)} \left(c_{\frac{n}{\mathcal{D}_l}}(d) \right)^{\kappa_l}.$$

□

3.4 SOME PROBLEMS

We close this chapter by proposing some problems for future work.

Problem 3.1. It seems that restricted linear congruences can be connected to the *zero-sum theory*. For example, Corollary 3.2.11 might lead to a new proof of the *Erdős–Ginzberg–Ziv Theorem with units* (see [3]). Studying the interactions between these areas seems an interesting problem.

Problem 3.2. What can we say about *restricted quadratic congruences*, the quadratic version of restricted linear congruences? Right now, there are only some partial results (for $k = 2$) available.

CHAPTER 4

Applications in Universal Hashing and Authentication with Secrecy

4.1 INTRODUCTION

Universal hash functions, discovered by Carter and Wegman [41], have many applications in computer science, including cryptography and information security [32, 59, 78, 80, 83, 84, 160, 196, 207], pseudorandomness [82, 151], complexity theory [164, 180], randomized algorithms [93, 146], data structures [153, 179], and parallel computing [98, 119, 161]. In this chapter, we connect restricted linear congruences to universal hashing. We introduce a variant of MMH*, that we call GRDH (Generalized Restricted Dot Product Hashing), where we use an arbitrary integer $n > 1$ instead of prime p and let the keys $\mathbf{x} = \langle x_1, \ldots, x_k \rangle \in \mathbb{Z}_n^k$ satisfy the conditions $(x_i, n) = t_i$ $(1 \le i \le k)$, where $t_1, \ldots, t_k$ are given positive divisors of n.

We investigate the universality of GRDH, and as an application of our results, we propose an authentication code with secrecy scheme.

Our results show that if one uses a composite integer n in the definition of MMH*, then even by choosing the keys $\mathbf{x} = \langle x_1, \ldots, x_k \rangle$ from $\mathbb{Z}_n^{*k}$, or, more generally, choosing the keys $\mathbf{x} = \langle x_1, \ldots, x_k \rangle$ from $\mathbb{Z}_n^k$ with the general conditions $(x_i, n) = t_i$ $(1 \leq i \leq k)$, where $t_1, \ldots, t_k$ are given positive divisors of n, we cannot get any strong collision bound (unless $k = 1$ and $(x_1, n) = t_1 = 1$; in this case, the collision probability for any two distinct messages is exactly zero). Such impossibility results were not known before.

We believe that connecting restricted linear congruences to universal hash functions is a novel idea and could be also of independent interest. A key ingredient in the proofs is Theorem 3.2.9, which gives an explicit formula for the number of solutions of restricted linear congruences (this theorem was proved in Chapter 3 using properties of Ramanujan sums and of the finite Fourier transform of arithmetic functions). So, we are actually building bridges between Ramanujan sums, finite Fourier transform, restricted linear congruences, and universal hashing. This approach might lead to further work.

4.2 GENERALIZED MULTILINEAR MODULAR HASHING

Given that, in the definition of MMH*, the modulus is a prime, it is natural to ask what happens if the modulus is an arbitrary integer $n > 1$. Is the resulting family, which we call GMMH* (Generalized Multilinear Modular Hashing), still Δ-universal? If not, what can we say about the ε-almost-universality or ε-almost-Δ-universality of this new family? This is an interesting and natural problem.

Definition 4.2.1. Let n and k be positive integers $(n > 1)$. The family GMMH* is defined as follows:

$$\text{GMMH}^* := \{h_\mathbf{x} \; : \; \mathbb{Z}_n^k \to \mathbb{Z}_n \mid \mathbf{x} \in \mathbb{Z}_n^k\}, \tag{4.2.1}$$

where

$$h_{\mathbf{x}}(\mathbf{m}) := \mathbf{m} \cdot \mathbf{x} \pmod{n} = \sum_{i=1}^{k} m_i x_i \pmod{n}, \qquad (4.2.2)$$

for any $\mathbf{x} = \langle x_1, \ldots, x_k \rangle \in \mathbb{Z}_n^k$ and any $\mathbf{m} = \langle m_1, \ldots, m_k \rangle \in \mathbb{Z}_n^k$.

MMH* has important applications; however, in applications that, for some reasons, we have to work in the ring $\mathbb{Z}_n$, the family GMMH* may be used.

Now, we state and prove the following result about the ε-almost-Δ-universality of GMMH*. Proposition 1.1.1, due to D. N. Lehmer [116], is the main ingredient in the proof.

Theorem 4.2.2. *Let n and k be positive integers ($n > 1$). The family GMMH* is $\frac{1}{p}$-AΔU, where p is the smallest prime divisor of n. This bound is tight.*

Proof. Suppose that n has the prime factorization $n = p_1^{r_1} \ldots p_s^{r_s}$, where $p_1 < \cdots < p_s$ are primes and $r_1, \ldots, r_s$ are positive integers. Let $\mathbf{m} = \langle m_1, \ldots, m_k \rangle \in \mathbb{Z}_n^k$ and $\mathbf{m}' = \langle m_1', \ldots, m_k' \rangle \in \mathbb{Z}_n^k$ be any two distinct messages. Put $\mathbf{a} = \langle a_1, \ldots, a_k \rangle = \mathbf{m} - \mathbf{m}'$. For every $b \in \mathbb{Z}_n$, we have

$$h_{\mathbf{x}}(\mathbf{m}) - h_{\mathbf{x}}(\mathbf{m}') = b \Longleftrightarrow \sum_{i=1}^{k} m_i x_i - \sum_{i=1}^{k} m_i' x_i \equiv b \pmod{n}$$

$$\Longleftrightarrow \sum_{i=1}^{k} a_i x_i \equiv b \pmod{n}.$$

Note that since $\langle x_1, \ldots, x_k \rangle \in \mathbb{Z}_n^k$, we have n^k ordered k-tuples $\langle x_1, \ldots, x_k \rangle$. Also, since $\mathbf{m} \neq \mathbf{m}'$, there exists some i_0 such that $a_{i_0} \neq 0$. Now, we need to find the maximum number of solutions of the linear congruence $\sum_{i=1}^{k} a_i x_i \equiv b \pmod{n}$ over all choices of $\mathbf{a} = \langle a_1, \ldots, a_k \rangle \in \mathbb{Z}_n^k \setminus \{\mathbf{0}\}$ and $b \in \mathbb{Z}_n$. By Proposition 1.1.1, if $\ell = (a_1, \ldots, a_k, n) \nmid b$, then the linear congruence $a_1 x_1 + \cdots + a_k x_k \equiv b \pmod{n}$ has no solution, and if $\ell = (a_1, \ldots, a_k, n) \mid b$, then the linear congruence has ℓn^{k-1} solutions. Thus, we need to find the maximum of $\ell = (a_1, \ldots, a_k, n)$ over all choices of $\mathbf{a} = \langle a_1, \ldots, a_k \rangle \in \mathbb{Z}_n^k \setminus \{\mathbf{0}\}$. Clearly,

$$\max_{\mathbf{a} = \langle a_1, \ldots, a_k \rangle \in \mathbb{Z}_n^k \setminus \{\mathbf{0}\}} (a_1, \ldots, a_k, n)$$

is achieved when $a_{i_0} = p_1^{r_1 - 1} p_2^{r_2} \ldots p_s^{r_s} = \frac{n}{p_1}$ and $a_i = 0$ $(i \neq i_0)$. So, we get

$$\max_{\mathbf{a} = \langle a_1, \ldots, a_k \rangle \in \mathbb{Z}_n^k \setminus \{\mathbf{0}\}} (a_1, \ldots, a_k, n) = p_1^{r_1 - 1} p_2^{r_2} \ldots p_s^{r_s} = \frac{n}{p_1}.$$

Therefore, for any two distinct messages $\mathbf{m}, \mathbf{m}' \in \mathbb{Z}_n^k$ and all $b \in \mathbb{Z}_n$, we have

$$\Pr{}_{h_{\mathbf{x}} \leftarrow \text{GMMH}^*} [h_{\mathbf{x}}(\mathbf{m}) - h_{\mathbf{x}}(\mathbf{m}') = b]$$

$$\leq \max_{\mathbf{a} = \langle a_1, \ldots, a_k \rangle \in \mathbb{Z}_n^k \setminus \{\mathbf{0}\}} \frac{n^{k-1}(a_1, \ldots, a_k, n)}{n^k} = \frac{1}{p_1}.$$

This means that GMMH* is $\frac{1}{p_1}$-AΔU. Clearly, this bound is tight; take, for example, $a_1 = \frac{n}{p_1}$ and $a_2 = \cdots = a_k = 0$. □

Corollary 4.2.3. *If in Theorem 4.2.2 we let n be a prime, then we obtain* Theorem 2.5.2.

Proof. When n is prime, $\gcd_{\mathbf{a} = \langle a_1, \ldots, a_k \rangle \in \mathbb{Z}_n^k \setminus \{\mathbf{0}\}} (a_1, \ldots, a_k, n) = 1$, so we get Δ-universality. □

We remark that if in the family GMMH* we let the keys $\mathbf{x} = \langle x_1, \ldots, x_k \rangle \in \mathbb{Z}_n^k$ satisfy the general conditions $(x_i, n) = t_i$ $(1 \leq i \leq k)$, where $t_1, \ldots, t_k$ are given positive divisors of n, then the resulting family, which we call GRDH, is no longer 'always' ε-AΔU; see the next section for details.

4.3 GRDH

In this section, we introduce a variant of MMH* that we call GRDH (Generalized Restricted Dot Product Hashing). Then, we investigate the ε-almost-universality and ε-almost-Δ-universality of GRDH via connecting the problem to the number of solutions of restricted linear congruences.

Definition 4.3.1. Let n and k be positive integers ($n > 1$). We define the family RDH (Restricted Dot Product Hashing) as follows:

$$\text{RDH} := \{\Upsilon_{\mathbf{x}} : \mathbb{Z}_n^k \to \mathbb{Z}_n : \mathbf{x} \in \mathbb{Z}_n^{*k}\}, \quad (4.3.1)$$

where

$$\Upsilon_{\mathbf{x}}(\mathbf{m}) := \mathbf{m} \cdot \mathbf{x} \quad (\text{mod } n) = \sum_{i=1}^{k} m_i x_i \quad (\text{mod } n), \quad (4.3.2)$$

for any $\mathbf{x} = \langle x_1, \ldots, x_k \rangle \in \mathbb{Z}_n^{*k}$ and any $\mathbf{m} = \langle m_1, \ldots, m_k \rangle \in \mathbb{Z}_n^k$. Suppose that $t_1, \ldots, t_k$ are given positive divisors of n. Now, if in the definition of RDH instead of having $\mathbf{x} = \langle x_1, \ldots, x_k \rangle \in \mathbb{Z}_n^{*k}$, we have, more generally, $\mathbf{x} = \langle x_1, \ldots, x_k \rangle \in \mathbb{Z}_n^k$ with $(x_i, n) = t_i$ ($1 \le i \le k$), then we get a generalization of RDH that we call GRDH.

It would be interesting to investigate for which values of n GRDH is ε-AU or ε-AΔU. We now deal with these problems. The explicit formula for the number of solutions of restricted linear congruences (Theorem 3.2.9) along with our approach for giving a generalization of Theorem 2.5.2 play key roles here.

First, we prove the following lemma that is needed in proving the main results.

Lemma 4.3.2. *Let k and n be positive integers ($n > 1$). For every prime divisor p of n, let r_p be the exponent of p in the prime factorization of n. Also, suppose that $t_1, \ldots, t_k$ are given positive divisors of n. There are the following two cases:*

(i) *If there exists some i_0 such that $t_{i_0} \neq 1$, then there exists $\mathbf{a} = \langle a_1, \ldots, a_k \rangle \in \mathbb{Z}_n^k \setminus \{\mathbf{0}\}$ such that for every prime $p \mid n$ we have $\mathfrak{m}_p(a_1, t_1, \ldots, a_k, t_k) > r_p$.*

(ii) *If $t_i = 1$ $(1 \leq i \leq k)$, then for every $\mathbf{a} = \langle a_1, \ldots, a_k \rangle \in \mathbb{Z}_n^k \setminus \{\mathbf{0}\}$, there exists at least one prime $p \mid n$ such that $\mathfrak{m}_p(a_1, \ldots, a_k) \leq r_p$.*

Proof. (i) Without loss of generality, let $t_1 \neq 1$, say, $t_1 = t$ with $t \mid n$ and $t > 1$. Take $a_1 = \frac{n}{t}$ and $a_2 = \cdots = a_k = 0$. Now, for every prime $p \mid n$ we have $p^{r_p} \mid a_i t_i$ $(1 \leq i \leq k)$. Therefore, for every prime $p \mid n$ we have $\mathfrak{m}_p(\frac{n}{t}, t, 0, t_2, \ldots, 0, t_k) > r_p$.

(ii) Let $t_i = 1$ $(1 \leq i \leq k)$ and $\mathbf{a} = \langle a_1, \ldots, a_k \rangle \in \mathbb{Z}_n^k \setminus \{\mathbf{0}\}$ be given. Suppose that for every prime $p \mid n$ we have $\mathfrak{m}_p(a_1, \ldots, a_k) > r_p$. This implies that for every prime $p \mid n$ we have $p^{r_p} \mid a_i$ $(1 \leq i \leq k)$. Therefore, we get $n \mid a_i$ $(1 \leq i \leq k)$, which is not possible because there exists some i such that $a_i \in \mathbb{Z}_n \setminus \{0\}$. $\square$

Now, we are ready to investigate the ε-almost-universality of GRDH.

Theorem 4.3.3. *Let n and k be positive integers $(n, k > 1)$. The family GRDH is an ε-AU family of hash functions for some $\varepsilon < 1$ if and only if n is odd and $(x_i, n) = t_i = 1$ $(1 \leq i \leq k)$. Furthermore, if these conditions are satisfied, then GRDH (which is then reduced to RDH) is $\frac{1}{p-1}$-AU, where p is the smallest prime divisor of n. This bound is tight.*

Proof. Assume the setting of the family GRDH, and assume that $\mathbf{t} = \langle t_1, \ldots, t_k \rangle$ is given. Let $n > 1$, and for every prime divisor p of n, let r_p be the exponent of p in the prime factorization of n. Suppose that $\mathbf{m} = \langle m_1, \ldots, m_k \rangle \in \mathbb{Z}_n^k$ and $\mathbf{m}' = \langle m_1', \ldots, m_k' \rangle \in \mathbb{Z}_n^k$ are any two distinct messages. Put $\mathbf{a} = \langle a_1, \ldots, a_k \rangle = \mathbf{m} - \mathbf{m}'$. Since $\mathbf{m} \neq \mathbf{m}'$, there exists some i such that $a_i \neq 0$. If in the family

GRDH there is a collision between $\mathbf{m}$ and $\mathbf{m'}$, this means that there exists an $\mathbf{x} = \langle x_1, \ldots, x_k \rangle \in \mathbb{Z}_n^k$ with $(x_i, n) = t_i$, $t_i \mid n$ $(1 \leq i \leq k)$ such that $\Upsilon_{\mathbf{x}}(\mathbf{m}) = \Upsilon_{\mathbf{x}}(\mathbf{m'})$. Clearly,

$$\Upsilon_{\mathbf{x}}(\mathbf{m}) = \Upsilon_{\mathbf{x}}(\mathbf{m'}) \iff \sum_{i=1}^{k} a_i x_i \equiv 0 \pmod{n}.$$

So, we need to find the number of solutions $\mathbf{x} = \langle x_1, \ldots, x_k \rangle \in \mathbb{Z}_n^k$ of the restricted linear congruence $a_1 x_1 + \cdots + a_k x_k \equiv 0 \pmod{n}$, with $(x_i, n) = t_i$, $t_i \mid n$ $(1 \leq i \leq k)$. Here, since $b = 0$, none of the two cases stated in the first part of Theorem 3.2.9 holds. Thus, by (3.2.11), there are exactly

$$\prod_{i=1}^{k} \varphi\left(\frac{n}{t_i}\right) \prod_{\substack{p \mid n \\ \mathfrak{m}_p \leq r_p}} p^{\mathfrak{m}_p - r_p - 1}\left(1 - \frac{(-1)^{e_p - 1}}{(p-1)^{e_p - 1}}\right) \tag{4.3.3}$$

choices for such $\mathbf{x} = \langle x_1, \ldots, x_k \rangle \in \mathbb{Z}_n^k$ that satisfy the aforementioned restricted linear congruence, where the last product is over the prime factors p of n with $\mathfrak{m}_p \leq r_p$, r_p is the exponent of p in the prime factorization of n, $\mathfrak{m}_p$ is the smallest $j \geq 1$ such that there is some i with $p^j \nmid a_i t_i$, and

$$e_p = \#\{i : 1 \leq i \leq k, p^{\mathfrak{m}_p} \nmid a_i t_i\}.$$

Also, since $(x_i, n) = t_i$ $(1 \leq i \leq k)$, the *total* number of choices for $\langle x_1, \ldots, x_k \rangle$ is $\prod_{i=1}^{k} \varphi(\frac{n}{t_i})$. Therefore, given any $\mathbf{a} = \langle a_1, \ldots, a_k \rangle \in \mathbb{Z}_n^k \setminus \{\mathbf{0}\}$, the collision probability is exactly

$$P_{\mathbf{a}}(n, \mathbf{t}) = \prod_{\substack{p \mid n \\ \mathfrak{m}_p \leq r_p}} p^{\mathfrak{m}_p - r_p - 1}\left(1 - \frac{(-1)^{e_p - 1}}{(p-1)^{e_p - 1}}\right). \tag{4.3.4}$$

Now, there are two cases:

(i) If for a prime $p \mid n$ we have $\mathfrak{m}_p \leq r_p$, then by (4.3.4) the term corresponding to this p in $P_{\mathbf{a}}(n, \mathbf{t})$ equals

$$p^{\mathfrak{m}_p - r_p - 1} \left(1 - \frac{(-1)^{e_p - 1}}{(p - 1)^{e_p - 1}} \right)$$

$$\leq p^{r_p - r_p - 1} \left(1 - \frac{(-1)^{2-1}}{(p - 1)^{2-1}} \right) = \frac{1}{p - 1}.$$

(ii) If for a prime $p \mid n$ we have $\mathfrak{m}_p > r_p$ then, by (4.3.4), the term corresponding to this p in $P_{\mathbf{a}}(n, \mathbf{t})$ equals 1.

Let there exists some i_0 such that $t_{i_0} \neq 1$. Then, by Lemma 4.3.2(i), there exists an $\mathbf{a} = \langle a_1, \ldots, a_k \rangle \in \mathbb{Z}_n^k \setminus \{\mathbf{0}\}$ such that for every prime $p \mid n$ we have $\mathfrak{m}_p(a_1, t_1, \ldots, a_k, t_k) > r_p$. Now, by (4.3.4) and case (ii), the collision probability for this specific $\mathbf{a}$ is *exactly one*. Thus, assume that $t_i = 1$ ($1 \leq i \leq k$). Then, if n is even, by taking $a_1 = a_2 = \frac{n}{2}$ and $a_3 = \cdots = a_k = 0$, one can see that $\mathfrak{m}_2(\frac{n}{2}, \frac{n}{2}, 0, \ldots, 0) = r_2$ and $e_2 = 2$, and for every other prime $p \mid n$ we have $\mathfrak{m}_p(\frac{n}{2}, \frac{n}{2}, 0, \ldots, 0) > r_p$. Now, by (4.3.4) and case (ii), the collision probability for this specific $\mathbf{a}$ is *exactly one*.

Next, suppose that n is odd and $t_i = 1$ ($1 \leq i \leq k$). Then, by Lemma 4.3.2(ii), for every $\mathbf{a} = \langle a_1, \ldots, a_k \rangle \in \mathbb{Z}_n^k \setminus \{\mathbf{0}\}$, there exists at least one prime $p \mid n$ such that $\mathfrak{m}_p(a_1, \ldots, a_k) \leq r_p$. Now, by (4.3.4) and cases (i) and (ii), one can see that

$$\max_{\mathbf{a} = \mathbf{m} - \mathbf{m}' \in \mathbb{Z}_n^k \setminus \{\mathbf{0}\}} P_{\mathbf{a}}(n, \mathbf{t})$$

is achieved in a specific $\mathbf{a} = \langle a_1, \ldots, a_k \rangle \in \mathbb{Z}_n^k \setminus \{\mathbf{0}\}$ for which there exists *exactly one* prime $p \mid n$ such that $\mathfrak{m}_p(a_1, \ldots, a_k) \leq r_p$, and furthermore, p has to be the smallest prime divisor of n, which we denote by $p_{\min}$.

Consequently, if n is odd and $(x_i, n) = t_i = 1$ $(1 \leq i \leq k)$, then for any two distinct messages $\mathbf{m}, \mathbf{m}' \in \mathbb{Z}_n^k$, we have

$$\Pr_{\Upsilon_\mathbf{x} \leftarrow \text{GRDH}}[\Upsilon_\mathbf{x}(\mathbf{m}) = \Upsilon_\mathbf{x}(\mathbf{m}')] \leq \max_{\mathbf{a} = \mathbf{m} - \mathbf{m}' \in \mathbb{Z}_n^k \setminus \{0\}}$$

$$P_\mathbf{a}(n, \mathbf{t}) \leq \frac{1}{p_{\min} - 1} \leq \frac{1}{2}.$$

Therefore, if n is odd and $(x_i, n) = t_i = 1$ $(1 \leq i \leq k)$, then GRDH (which is then reduced to RDH) is $\frac{1}{p_{\min}-1}$-AU. We also note that this bound is tight: Take $a_1 = a_2 = \frac{n}{p_{\min}}$ and $a_3 = \cdots = a_k = 0$. Then, we get that $\mathbf{m}_{p_{\min}}(\frac{n}{p_{\min}}, \frac{n}{p_{\min}}, 0, \ldots, 0) = r_{p_{\min}}$ and $e_{p_{\min}} = 2$, and for every other prime $p \mid n$, we get that $\mathbf{m}_p(\frac{n}{p_{\min}}, \frac{n}{p_{\min}}, 0, \ldots, 0) > r_p$. Now, by (4.3.4) and case (ii), the collision probability for this specific $\mathbf{a}$ is *exactly* $\frac{1}{p_{\min}-1} \leq \frac{1}{2}$. □

The following remark gives a necessary and sufficient condition for the ε-almost-universality of the family GRDH in the case of $k = 1$. We omit the proof as it is simply obtained from the previous argument (this special case can also be proved directly).

Remark 4.3.4. *If $k = 1$, then the family GRDH is an ε-AU family of hash functions for some $\varepsilon < 1$ if and only if $(x_1, n) = t_1 = 1$. Furthermore, if $(x_1, n) = t_1 = 1$, then the collision probability for any two distinct messages is exactly zero.*

Now, we investigate the ε-almost-Δ-universality of GRDH. Note the change from $k > 1$ in Theorem 4.3.3 to $k \geq 1$ in Theorem 4.3.5. The proof idea is similar to that of Theorem 4.3.3; so, in the proof we only write the parts that need more arguments.

Theorem 4.3.5. *Let n and k be positive integers $(n > 1)$. The family GRDH is an ε-AΔU family of hash functions for some $\varepsilon < 1$ if and only if n is odd and $(x_i, n) = t_i = 1$ $(1 \leq i \leq k)$. Furthermore, if these conditions are satisfied, then GRDH (which is then reduced to RDH) is $\frac{1}{p-1}$-AΔU, where p is the smallest prime divisor of n. This bound is tight.*

Proof. Assume the setting of the family GRDH, and assume that $\mathbf{t} = \langle t_1, \ldots, t_k \rangle$ is given. Let $n > 1$, and for every prime divisor p of n, let r_p be the exponent of p in the prime factorization of n. If for a given $\mathbf{a} = \langle a_1, \ldots, a_k \rangle \in \mathbb{Z}_n^k \setminus \{0\}$ and a given $b \in \mathbb{Z}_n$, there is a prime $p \mid n$ such that $\mathfrak{m}_p \leq r_p$ and $p^{\mathfrak{m}_p - 1} \nmid b$, or such that $\mathfrak{m}_p \geq r_p + 1$ and $p^{r_p} \nmid b$, then, by the first part of Theorem 3.2.9, the probability that we have $\Upsilon_{\mathbf{x}}(\mathbf{m}) - \Upsilon_{\mathbf{x}}(\mathbf{m'}) = b$ is *exactly zero*. Otherwise, given any $\mathbf{a} = \langle a_1, \ldots, a_k \rangle \in \mathbb{Z}_n^k \setminus \{0\}$ and any $b \in \mathbb{Z}_n$, the probability that we have $\Upsilon_{\mathbf{x}}(\mathbf{m}) - \Upsilon_{\mathbf{x}}(\mathbf{m'}) = b$ is exactly

$$Q_{\mathbf{a},b}(n, \mathbf{t}) = \prod_{\substack{p \mid n \\ \mathfrak{m}_p \leq r_p \\ p^{\mathfrak{m}_p} \mid b}} p^{\mathfrak{m}_p - r_p - 1} \left(1 - \frac{(-1)^{e_p - 1}}{(p-1)^{e_p - 1}} \right)$$

$$\prod_{\substack{p \mid n \\ \mathfrak{m}_p \leq r_p \\ p^{\mathfrak{m}_p - 1} \parallel b}} p^{\mathfrak{m}_p - r_p - 1} \left(1 - \frac{(-1)^{e_p}}{(p-1)^{e_p}} \right). \qquad (4.3.5)$$

Now, there are three cases:

(i) If for a prime $p \mid n$ we have $\mathfrak{m}_p \leq r_p$ and $p^{\mathfrak{m}_p - 1} \parallel b$, then, by (4.3.5), the term corresponding to this p in $Q_{\mathbf{a},b}(n, \mathbf{t})$ equals

$$p^{\mathfrak{m}_p - r_p - 1} \left(1 - \frac{(-1)^{e_p}}{(p-1)^{e_p}} \right) \leq p^{r_p - r_p - 1} \left(1 - \frac{(-1)^1}{(p-1)^1} \right)$$

$$= \frac{1}{p-1}.$$

(ii) If for a prime $p \mid n$ we have $\mathfrak{m}_p \leq r_p$ and $p^{\mathfrak{m}_p} \mid b$, then, by (4.3.5), the term corresponding to this p in $Q_{\mathbf{a},b}(n, \mathbf{t})$ equals

$$p^{\mathfrak{m}_p - r_p - 1} \left(1 - \frac{(-1)^{e_p - 1}}{(p-1)^{e_p - 1}} \right) \leq p^{r_p - r_p - 1} \left(1 - \frac{(-1)^{2 - 1}}{(p-1)^{2 - 1}} \right)$$

$$= \frac{1}{p-1}.$$

(iii) If for a prime $p \mid n$ we have $m_p > r_p$ and $p^{r_p} \mid b$, then, by (4.3.5), the term corresponding to this p in $Q_{a,b}(n, \mathbf{t})$ equals one.

If there exists some i_0 such that $t_{i_0} \neq 1$, then the argument is exactly the same as before (just take $b = 0$). Now, assume that $t_i = 1$ $(1 \leq i \leq k)$. Then, if n is even, take $a_1 = b = \frac{n}{2}$ and $a_2 = \cdots = a_k = 0$. Now, one can see that, by (4.3.5) and case (iii), the probability that we have $\Upsilon_x(\mathbf{m}) - \Upsilon_x(\mathbf{m}') = b$ for these specific $\mathbf{a}$ and b is *exactly one*.

Now, suppose that n is odd and $t_i = 1$ $(1 \leq i \leq k)$. Then, by (4.3.5), Lemma 4.3.2(ii), and cases (i), (ii), and (iii), one can see that

$$\max_{\substack{\mathbf{a} = \mathbf{m} - \mathbf{m}' \in \mathbb{Z}_n^k \setminus \{\mathbf{0}\} \\ b \in \mathbb{Z}_n}} Q_{a,b}(n, \mathbf{t})$$

is achieved in a specific $\mathbf{a} = \langle a_1, \ldots, a_k \rangle \in \mathbb{Z}_n^k \setminus \{\mathbf{0}\}$ and a specific $b \in \mathbb{Z}_n$ for which there exists *exactly one* prime $p \mid n$ such that $m_p(a_1, \ldots, a_k) \leq r_p$ and $p^{m_p - 1} \| b$, or $m_p(a_1, \ldots, a_k) \leq r_p$ and $p^{m_p} \mid b$, and also $p^{r_p} \mid b$ for every other prime $p \mid n$; furthermore, p has to be the smallest prime divisor of n that we denote by $p_{\min}$.

Consequently, if n is odd and $(x_i, n) = t_i = 1$ $(1 \leq i \leq k)$, then for any two distinct messages $\mathbf{m}, \mathbf{m}' \in \mathbb{Z}_n^k$, and all $b \in \mathbb{Z}_n$, we have

$$\Pr_{\Upsilon_x \leftarrow \text{GRDH}}[\Upsilon_x(\mathbf{m}) - \Upsilon_x(\mathbf{m}') = b] \leq \max_{\substack{\mathbf{a} = \mathbf{m} - \mathbf{m}' \in \mathbb{Z}_n^k \setminus \{\mathbf{0}\} \\ b \in \mathbb{Z}_n}} Q_{a,b}(n, \mathbf{t})$$

$$\leq \frac{1}{p_{\min} - 1} \leq \frac{1}{2}.$$

Therefore, if n is odd and $(x_i, n) = t_i = 1$ $(1 \leq i \leq k)$, then GRDH (which is then reduced to RDH) is $\frac{1}{p_{\min} - 1}$-A$\triangle$U. We also note that this bound is tight: Take $a_1 = b = \frac{n}{p_{\min}}$ and $a_2 = \cdots = a_k = 0$. Now, by (4.3.5) and case (iii), one can see that the probability that we have $\Upsilon_x(\mathbf{m}) - \Upsilon_x(\mathbf{m'}) = b$ for these specific $\mathbf{a}$ and b is *exactly* $\frac{1}{p_{\min}-1}$. □

Remark 4.3.6. *Though the proofs of Theorem 4.3.3 and Theorem 4.3.5 are simple thanks to Theorem 3.2.9, there may be simpler proofs (say, without relying on the counting arguments as we do) for these results. However, given the general statements of Theorem 4.3.3 and Theorem 4.3.5, possible simpler proofs for these results that cover the 'whole' statements may not be necessarily that much shorter. Besides, we believe that our proof techniques have their own merit and these connections and techniques may motivate more work in universal hashing and related areas.*

Remark 4.3.7. *If in Theorem 4.3.5 we let $k = 1$, then we get the main result of the paper by Alomair et al. [7, Th. 5.11], which was obtained via a very long argument.*

Remark 4.3.8. *Using Theorem 3.2.9 and the idea of the proof of Theorem 4.3.5, one can see that there are cases in which the collision probability in the family GRDH is exactly zero (Corollary 3.2.11 completely characterizes these cases). This can be considered an advantage of the family GRDH and is not the case in the family MMH*, as the collision probability in MMH* is exactly $\frac{1}{p}$, which never vanishes.*

4.4 APPLICATIONS TO AUTHENTICATION WITH SECRECY

As an application of the results of the preceding section, we propose an authentication code with secrecy scheme that generalizes a recent construction [7, 9]. We remark that Alomair et al. have applied their scheme in several other papers; see, e.g., [8] for an application of this approach in the authentication problem in radio frequency identification systems. So, our results may have implications in those applications, as well. We adopt the notation of [134] in specifying the syntax of these codes. In particular, we consider key-indexed families of coding rules.

An *authentication code with secrecy* (or *code* for short) is a tuple $C = (S, M, K, \mathcal{E}, D)$, specified by the following sets: S of *source states* (or *plaintexts*), M of *messages* (or *ciphertexts*), K of *keys*, $\mathcal{E}$ of *authenticated encryption (AE) functions*, and D of *verified decryption functions*. The sets $\mathcal{E}$ and D are indexed by K. For $k \in K$, $\mathcal{E}_k : S \to M$ is the associated authenticated encryption function and $D_k : M \to S \cup \{\perp\}$ is the associated verified decryption function. The encryption and decryption functions have the property that, for every $m \in S$, $D_k(\mathcal{E}_k(m)) = m$. Moreover, for any $c \in M$, if $c \neq \mathcal{E}_k(m)$ for some $m \in S$, $D_k(c) = \perp$.

Before presenting our construction, we first note that although it is not explicitly stated in [7] or [9], the construction given there is correct only for the case of a uniform distribution on source states. This will be the case for our construction, as well. We note that this assumption, though unrealistically strong from a security perspective, is commonly used in the study of authentication codes with secrecy. Following the terminology of [91] (see also [92]), we will call such codes *authentication and secrecy codes for equiprobable source probability distributions*. Henceforth, we will work under the assumption of equiprobable source states.

We now give the security definitions required for authentication and secrecy. We begin with a definition of secrecy.

Definition 4.4.1. We say that $C = (S, M, K, \mathcal{E}, D)$ provides *ε-secrecy* on $S' \subseteq S$ if, for every $m \in S'$ and $c \in M$,

$$\Pr_{m' \leftarrow S, k \leftarrow K} [m' = m | \mathcal{E}_k(m') = c] \leq \varepsilon.$$

Thus, $\frac{1}{|S|}$-secrecy on S corresponds to the standard notion of Shannon secrecy [177] (for a uniform message distribution).

With respect to authentication, we restrict attention to *substitution attacks*, also known as *spoofing attacks of order* 1. A C-*forger* is a mapping $\mathcal{F} : M \to M$. Note that there are no computational restrictions on $\mathcal{F}$. We say that C is δ-*secure against substitution attacks* if for every C-forger $\mathcal{F}$

$$\Pr_{m \leftarrow \mathcal{S}, k \leftarrow \mathcal{K}, c \leftarrow \mathcal{E}_k(m)} [\mathcal{F}(c) \neq c \wedge \mathcal{D}_k(\mathcal{F}(c)) \neq \perp] \leq \delta.$$

Finally, we say that C is an ε, δ-*authentication code with secrecy for equiprobable source states* on $\mathcal{S}'$ if it is ε-secret on $\mathcal{S}'$ and δ-secure against substitution attacks.

For any $n, k \in \mathbb{N}$, we define $C_{RDH}^{n,k}$ as follows: $\mathcal{S} = \mathbb{Z}_n^k$, $\mathcal{K} = \mathbb{Z}_n^k \times (\mathbb{Z}_n^*)^k$, $\mathcal{M} = \mathbb{Z}_n^k \times \mathbb{Z}_n$. Thus, source states are k-tuples $\mathbf{m} = \langle m_1, \ldots, m_k \rangle$, keys are pairs $\langle \mathbf{x}, \mathbf{y} \rangle$ of k-tuples $\mathbf{x} = \langle x_1, \ldots, x_k \rangle$, $\mathbf{y} = \langle y_1, \ldots, y_k \rangle$, and ciphertexts are pairs $\langle \mathbf{c}, t \rangle$.

Note that we will sometimes write pairs using the notation $\cdot || \cdot$ rather than the usual $\langle \cdot, \cdot \rangle$, e.g., we write a key pair as $\mathbf{x} || \mathbf{y}$. Also, we may abuse terminology and for a ciphertext $\mathbf{c} || t$, call $\mathbf{c}$ the ciphertext and t the *tag*. The authenticated encryption function $\mathcal{E}$ is defined as follows:

$$\mathcal{E}_{\mathbf{x} || \mathbf{y}}(\mathbf{m}) = \Psi_{\mathbf{x}}(\mathbf{m}) || \Upsilon_{\mathbf{y}}(\mathbf{m}),$$

where Υ is the RDH hash function and

$$\Psi_{\mathbf{x}}(\mathbf{m}) = \mathbf{m} + \mathbf{x} \pmod{n} = \langle m_1 + x_1 \pmod{n}, \ldots, m_k + x_k$$
$$\pmod{n} \rangle.$$

To define $\mathcal{D}$, we first define Ψ^{-1}:

$$\Psi_{\mathbf{x}}^{-1}(\mathbf{c}) = \mathbf{c} - \mathbf{x} \pmod{n} = \langle c_1 - x_1 \pmod{n}, \ldots, c_k - x_k$$
$$\pmod{n} \rangle.$$

Then,

$$\mathcal{D}_{\mathbf{x} || \mathbf{y}}(\mathbf{c} || t) = \begin{cases} \Psi_{\mathbf{x}}^{-1}(\mathbf{c}), & \text{if } \Upsilon_{\mathbf{y}}(\Psi_{\mathbf{x}}^{-1}(\mathbf{c})) = t, \\ \perp, & \text{otherwise.} \end{cases}$$

Now, we are ready to state and prove our main result in this section.

Theorem 4.4.2. *Let $n, k \in \mathbb{N}$, where n is odd, and let p be the smallest prime divisor of n. Then, $\mathrm{C}_{\mathrm{RDH}}^{n,k}$ is a $\frac{1}{(p-1)n^{k-1}}, \frac{1}{p-1}$-authentication code with secrecy for equiprobable source states on $\mathbb{Z}_n^k \setminus \{0\}$.*

We will establish this theorem by the following sequence of lemmas.

Lemma 4.4.3. *Let $n, k \in \mathbb{N}$, where n is odd, and let p be the smallest prime divisor of n. Then, $\mathrm{C}_{\mathrm{RDH}}^{n,k}$ is $\frac{1}{(p-1)n^{k-1}}$-secret on $\mathbb{Z}_n^k \setminus \{0\}$.*

Proof. We first note that for any $\mathbf{m}$, $\mathbf{c}$, and t,

$$\Pr_{\mathbf{m}', \mathbf{x} \leftarrow \mathbb{Z}_n^k, \mathbf{y} \leftarrow (\mathbb{Z}_n^*)^k} [\mathbf{m}' = \mathbf{m} | \mathcal{E}_{\mathbf{x} \| \mathbf{y}}(\mathbf{m}') = \mathbf{c} \| t]$$

$$= \Pr_{\mathbf{m}' \leftarrow \mathbb{Z}_n^k, \mathbf{y} \leftarrow (\mathbb{Z}_n^*)^k} [\mathbf{m}' = \mathbf{m} | \Upsilon_{\mathbf{y}}(\mathbf{m}') = t].$$

This follows from the independence of $\Psi_{\mathbf{x}}(\mathbf{m}')$ and $\Upsilon_{\mathbf{y}}(\mathbf{m}')$, conditioned on $\mathbf{m}' = \mathbf{m}$, along with the fact that Ψ provides Shannon secrecy. But,

$$\Pr_{\mathbf{m}' \leftarrow \mathbb{Z}_n^k, \mathbf{y} \leftarrow (\mathbb{Z}_n^*)^k} [\mathbf{m}' = \mathbf{m} | \Upsilon_{\mathbf{y}}(\mathbf{m}') = t]$$

$$= \Pr_{\mathbf{m}' \leftarrow \mathbb{Z}_n^k, \mathbf{y} \leftarrow (\mathbb{Z}_n^*)^k} \frac{[\Upsilon_{\mathbf{y}}(\mathbf{m}') = t | \mathbf{m}' = \mathbf{m}]}{n^{k-1}}$$

$$\leq \frac{1}{(p-1)n^{k-1}},$$

where the equality follows by Bayes' rule and the fact that for $\mathbf{m}' \leftarrow (\mathbb{Z}_n)^k$ and $\mathbf{y} \leftarrow (\mathbb{Z}_n^*)^k$, $\Upsilon_{\mathbf{y}}(\mathbf{m}')$ is uniformly distributed in $\mathbb{Z}_n$, and the inequality follows, assuming $\mathbf{m} \neq \mathbf{0}$, by Theorem 4.3.5. $\qquad\square$

We now establish a *key hiding* property that will be needed to prove resistance to substitution attacks.

Lemma 4.4.4. *For* $n, k \in \mathbb{N}$, $\mathbf{y} \in (\mathbb{Z}_n^*)^k$, $\mathbf{c} \in \mathbb{Z}_n^k$, *and* $t \in \mathbb{Z}_n$,

$$\Pr_{\mathbf{x}, \mathbf{m} \in \mathbb{Z}_n^k, \mathbf{y}' \in (\mathbb{Z}_n^*)^k} [\mathbf{y}' = \mathbf{y} | \mathcal{E}_{\mathbf{x} || \mathbf{y}'}(\mathbf{m}) = \mathbf{c} || t] = \frac{1}{|(\mathbb{Z}_n^*)^k|}.$$

Proof. First, note that since $\mathbf{x}$ and $\mathbf{m}$ are chosen independently of $\mathbf{y}'$, it is the case that $\Psi_{\mathbf{x}}(\mathbf{m})$ and $\mathbf{y}'$ are independent. So, we just need to show that

$$\Pr_{\mathbf{m} \in \mathbb{Z}_n^k, \mathbf{y}' \in (\mathbb{Z}_n^*)^k} [\mathbf{y}' = \mathbf{y} | \Upsilon_{\mathbf{y}'}(\mathbf{m}) = t] = \frac{1}{|(\mathbb{Z}_n^*)^k|}.$$

Note that

$$\Pr_{\mathbf{m} \in \mathbb{Z}_n^k, \mathbf{y}' \in (\mathbb{Z}_n^*)^k} [\Upsilon_{\mathbf{y}'}(\mathbf{m}) = t | \mathbf{y}' = \mathbf{y}]$$

$$= \Pr_{\mathbf{m} \in \mathbb{Z}_n^k, \mathbf{y}' \in (\mathbb{Z}_n^*)^k} [\Upsilon_{\mathbf{y}'}(\mathbf{m}) = t \wedge \mathbf{y}' = \mathbf{y}] / \Pr_{\mathbf{y}' \in (\mathbb{Z}_n^*)^k} [\mathbf{y}' = \mathbf{y}]$$

$$= \Pr_{\mathbf{m} \in \mathbb{Z}_n^k, \mathbf{y}' \in (\mathbb{Z}_n^*)^k} [\Upsilon_{\mathbf{y}}(\mathbf{m}) = t \wedge \mathbf{y}' = \mathbf{y}] / \Pr_{\mathbf{y}' \in (\mathbb{Z}_n^*)^k} [\mathbf{y}' = \mathbf{y}]$$

$$= \Pr_{\mathbf{m} \in \mathbb{Z}_n^k} [\Upsilon_{\mathbf{y}}(\mathbf{m}) = t] \cdot \Pr_{\mathbf{y}' \in (\mathbb{Z}_n^*)^k} [\mathbf{y}' = \mathbf{y}] / \Pr_{\mathbf{y}' \in (\mathbb{Z}_n^*)^k} [\mathbf{y}' = \mathbf{y}]$$

$$= \Pr_{\mathbf{m} \in \mathbb{Z}_n^k} [\Upsilon_{\mathbf{y}}(\mathbf{m}) = t] = \frac{1}{|\mathbb{Z}_n|},$$

where the last equality follows because the product of a uniformly random element of $\mathbb{Z}_n$ and a fixed element of $\mathbb{Z}_n^*$ is uniformly distributed in $\mathbb{Z}_n$, and the sum of a fixed number of uniformly random elements of $\mathbb{Z}_n$ is uniformly distributed in $\mathbb{Z}_n$. We now have

$$\Pr_{\mathbf{m}\in\mathbb{Z}_n^k,\mathbf{y}'\in(\mathbb{Z}_n^*)^k}[\mathbf{y}' = \mathbf{y}|\Upsilon_{\mathbf{y}'}(\mathbf{m}) = t]$$

$$= \Pr_{\mathbf{m}\in\mathbb{Z}_n^k,\mathbf{y}'\in(\mathbb{Z}_n^*)^k}[\Upsilon_{\mathbf{y}'}(\mathbf{m}) = t|\mathbf{y}' = \mathbf{y}]\cdot$$

$$\frac{\Pr_{\mathbf{y}'\in(\mathbb{Z}_n^*)^k}[\mathbf{y}' = \mathbf{y}]}{\Pr_{\mathbf{m}\in\mathbb{Z}_n^k,\mathbf{y}'\in(\mathbb{Z}_n^*)^k}[\Upsilon_{\mathbf{y}'}(\mathbf{m}) = t]}. \quad (4.4.1)$$

But,

$$\Pr_{\mathbf{m}\in\mathbb{Z}_n^k,\mathbf{y}'\in(\mathbb{Z}_n^*)^k}[\Upsilon_{\mathbf{y}'}(\mathbf{m}) = t]$$

$$= \sum_{\mathbf{y}\in(\mathbb{Z}_n^*)^k}\Pr_{\mathbf{m}\in\mathbb{Z}_n^k,\mathbf{y}'\in(\mathbb{Z}_n^*)^k}[\Upsilon_{\mathbf{y}'}(\mathbf{m}) = t|\mathbf{y}' = \mathbf{y}]\cdot\Pr_{\mathbf{y}'\in(\mathbb{Z}_n^*)^k}[\mathbf{y}' = \mathbf{y}]$$

$$= \frac{1}{|\mathbb{Z}_n|}.$$

Combining this with (4.4.1) completes the proof. $\square$

Remark 4.4.5. *This key hiding property does not hold in general. The given proof depends on the fact that* **m** *is uniformly distributed in* $\mathbb{Z}_n^k$.

Lemma 4.4.6. *Let* $n, k \in \mathbb{N}$, *where* n *is odd, and let* p *be the smallest prime divisor of* n. *Then,* $C_{RDH}^{n,k}$ *is* $\frac{1}{p-1}$-*secure against substitution attacks.*

Proof. By way of contradiction, suppose that $\mathcal{F}$ produces a substitution with probability greater than $\frac{1}{p-1}$. By averaging, there must be some $\mathbf{m} \in \mathbb{Z}_n^k$ such that if $\mathcal{E}_{\mathbf{x}||\mathbf{y}}(\mathbf{m}) = \mathbf{c}||t$, for random $\mathbf{x}$ and $\mathbf{y}$, then $\mathcal{F}(\mathbf{c}||t) = \mathbf{c}'||t'$ such that $\mathbf{c}'||t' \neq \mathbf{c}||t$ and $\Upsilon_{\mathbf{y}}(\Phi_{\mathbf{x}}^{-1})(\mathbf{c}') = t'$. Let $b = t - t'$ and $\mathbf{m}' = (\Phi_{\mathbf{x}}^{-1})(\mathbf{c}')$. Note that it must be the case that $\mathbf{m}' \neq \mathbf{m}$. By the preceding lemma, $\mathbf{y}$ and $\mathbf{m}'$ are statistically independent. So,

$$\Upsilon_{\mathbf{y}}(\mathbf{m}) - \Upsilon_{\mathbf{y}}(\mathbf{m}') = b,$$

for randomly chosen $\mathbf{y} \in (\mathbb{Z}_n^*)^k$, violating that RDH is $\frac{1}{p-1}$-AΔU by Theorem 4.3.5. □

4.5 DISCUSSION

The proposed scheme, which is a generalization of the scheme proposed by [7] and [9], is defined using the *encrypt-and-authenticate* paradigm (see [16, 110] and the references therein for a detailed discussion about these generic constructions and their security analysis). Since this approach requires the decryption of a purported ciphertext before its authentication, it is susceptible to attacks if the implementation of the decryption function leaks information when given invalid ciphertexts. Surprisingly, the preferred *encrypt-then-authenticate* approach will not work in our setting because it does not have key hiding.

We now show that the assumption that messages are generated uniformly at random is necessary for our result, by showing that any authentication scheme achieving ε-security against substitution attacks for arbitrary source distributions is in fact an ε-ASU hash family.

We begin with some definitions.

Definition 4.5.1. An *authentication code* is specified by a tuple $M = (\mathcal{S}, \mathcal{T}, \mathcal{K}, \mathcal{M}, \mathcal{V})$, where $\mathcal{S}$ is the set of *source states*, $\mathcal{T}$ is the set of *tags*, $\mathcal{K}$ is the set of *keys*, $\mathcal{M} : \mathcal{K} \times \mathcal{S} \to \mathcal{T}$, and $\mathcal{V} : \mathcal{K} \times \mathcal{T} \to \{0, 1\}$. It must be the case that for all $k \in \mathcal{K}$ and $m \in \mathcal{S}$, $\mathcal{V}_k(m||\mathcal{M}_k(m)) = 1$. A *forger* is a mapping $\mathcal{F} = \langle \mathcal{F}_1, \mathcal{F}_2 \rangle$, where $\mathcal{F}_1 : \mathcal{S} \times \mathcal{T} \to \mathcal{S}$ and $\mathcal{F}_2 : \mathcal{S} \times \mathcal{T} \to \mathcal{T}$. We say M is *$\varepsilon$-secure against substitution attacks* if for every forger $\mathcal{F}$ and distribution

Universal Hashing and Authentication with Secrecy ■ 69

S on $\mathcal{S}$,

$$\Pr_{\substack{k\leftarrow\mathcal{K},m\leftarrow_s\mathcal{S}\\t\leftarrow\mathcal{M}_k(m)}}[\mathcal{F}_1(m,t)\neq m\wedge\mathcal{V}_k(\mathcal{F}(m\|t))=1]\leq\varepsilon.$$

Theorem 4.5.2. *Suppose that* $M=(\mathcal{S},\mathcal{T},\mathcal{K},\mathcal{M},\mathcal{V})$ *is* ε-*secure against substitution attacks. Then,* $\{\mathcal{M}_k\mid k\in\mathcal{K}\}$ *is an* ε-ASU *hash function family.*

Proof. Suppose that $\{\mathcal{M}_k\mid k\in\mathcal{K}\}$ is not an ε-ASU hash family. So, there are $m'\neq m''\in\mathcal{S}$ and $t',t''\in\mathcal{T}$ such that $\Pr_{k\leftarrow\mathcal{K}}[\mathcal{M}_k(m'')=t''\wedge\mathcal{M}_k(m')=t']>\varepsilon$. Take $\mathcal{F}$ such that $\mathcal{F}(m'\|t')=m''\|t''$, and let S be the distribution on $\mathcal{S}$ that puts all weight on m'. Then,

$$\Pr_{\substack{k\leftarrow\mathcal{K},m\leftarrow_s\mathcal{S}\\t\leftarrow\mathcal{M}_k(m)}}[\mathcal{F}_1(m,t)\neq m\wedge\mathcal{V}_k(\mathcal{F}(m\|t))=1]$$

$$=\Pr_{\substack{k\leftarrow\mathcal{K}\\t\leftarrow\mathcal{M}_k(m')}}[\mathcal{F}_1(m',t)\neq m'\wedge\mathcal{V}_k(\mathcal{F}(m'\|t))=1]$$

$$=\Pr_{\substack{k\leftarrow\mathcal{K}\\t\leftarrow\mathcal{M}_k(m')}}[\mathcal{F}_1(m',t)\neq m'\wedge\mathcal{V}_k(\mathcal{F}(m'\|t))=1\mid t=t']$$

$$\cdot\Pr_{\substack{k\leftarrow\mathcal{K}\\t\leftarrow\mathcal{M}_k(m')}}[t=t']$$

$$=\Pr_{k\leftarrow\mathcal{K}}[\mathcal{F}_1(m',t')\neq m'\wedge\mathcal{V}_k(\mathcal{F}(m'\|t'))=1\wedge\mathcal{M}_k(m')=t']$$

$$=\Pr_{k\leftarrow\mathcal{K}}[m''\neq m'\wedge\mathcal{M}_k(m'')=t''\wedge\mathcal{M}_k(m')=t']>\varepsilon.$$

$\square$

Problem 4.1. So far, we have mentioned an application of GRDH in cryptography. As universal hash functions have many applications in computer science, it would be an interesting question to investigate other areas where GMMH* and GRDH are of possible interest.

CHAPTER 5

Applications in String Theory and Quantum Field Theory

5.1 INTRODUCTION

A *surface* is a compact oriented two-dimensional topological manifold. Roughly speaking, a surface is a space that 'locally' looks like the Euclidean plane. Informally, a graph is said to be *embedded into* (or *drawn on*) a surface if it can be drawn on the surface in such a way that its edges meet only at their endpoints. A *ribbon graph* is a finite and connected graph together with a cyclic ordering on the set of half edges incident to each vertex. One can see that ribbon graphs and embedded graphs are essentially equivalent concepts; that is, a ribbon graph can be thought of as a set of disks (or vertices) attached to each other by thin stripes (or edges) glued to their boundaries. There are several other names for these graphs in the literature, for example, *fat graphs*, *combinatorial maps*, and *unrooted maps*. For a thorough introduction to the theory of embedded graphs, we refer the reader to the lovely book by Lando and Zvonkin [113].

The many important applications of graphs embedded into surfaces include ribbon graphs and their counting, which, as previously mentioned, is of great interest in string theory and QFT. Here, we quote some of these applications and motivations from [105] and [106]:

- Ribbon graphs arise in the context of MHV (maximally helicity violating) rules for constructing amplitudes. In the MHV rules approach to amplitudes, inspired by twistor string theory, amplitudes are constructed by gluing MHV vertices. Counting ribbon graphs plays an important role here in finding different ways of gluing the vertices that contribute to a given amplitude.

- The number of ribbon graphs is the fundamental combinatorial element in perturbative large N QFT computations, since we need to be able to enumerate the graphs and then compute corresponding Feynman integrals.

- In matrix models (more specifically, the Gaussian Hermitian and complex matrix models), which can be viewed as QFTs in zero dimensions, the correlators are related very closely to the combinatorics of ribbon graphs. There is also a two-dimensional structure (related to string worldsheets) to this combinatorics.

- There is a bijection between vacuum graphs of quantum electrodynamics (QED) and ribbon graphs. In fact, the number of QED/Yukawa vacuum graphs with $2v$ vertices is equal to the number of ribbon graphs with v edges. This can be proved using permutations. Note that QED is an Abelian gauge theory with the symmetry circle group $U(1)$.

Mednykh and Nedela [137] obtained a formula for the number of unrooted maps of a given genus. Recently, Koch et al. [106] gave a refinement of this formula to make it more suitable for applications to several physics problems, such as the ones mentioned here. In both formulas, there is an important factor, namely, the number of surface-kernel epimorphisms from a co-compact Fuchsian group to a cyclic group. A formula for the number of such epimorphisms is given by [137], but it does not seem to be very applicable, especially for large values, because one needs to find, as part of the formula, a challenging summation involving the products of some Ramanujan sums and for each index of summation, one needs to calculate these products. The aim of this chapter is to give a very explicit and practical formula for the number of such epimorphisms. Our formula does not contain Ramanujan sums or other challenging parts, and is easy to work with. As a consequence, we obtain an 'equivalent' form of the famous Harvey theorem on the cyclic groups of automorphisms of compact Riemann surfaces.

Our main result is presented in Section 5.2. A key ingredient in the proofs is Theorem 3.2.9, which gives an explicit formula for the number of solutions of restricted linear congruences (this theorem was proved in Chapter 3 using properties of Ramanujan sums and of the finite Fourier transform of arithmetic functions).

5.2 COUNTING SURFACE-KERNEL EPIMORPHISMS FROM Γ TO $\mathbb{Z}_N$

In this section, we obtain an explicit formula for the number of surface-kernel epimorphisms from a co-compact Fuchsian group to a cyclic group. Then, we give an example and also some applications.

Theorem 5.2.1. *Let Γ be a co-compact Fuchsian group with signature $(g; n_1, \ldots, n_k)$, and let $\mathfrak{n} := \mathrm{lcm}(n_1, \ldots, n_k)$. If $\mathfrak{n} \nmid n$ then there is no surface-kernel epimorphism from Γ to $\mathbb{Z}_n$. Otherwise, the* *number of surface-kernel epimorphisms from Γ to $\mathbb{Z}_n$ is*

$$|\mathrm{Epi}_S(\Gamma, \mathbb{Z}_n)| = \frac{n^{2g}}{n} \prod_{i=1}^{k} \varphi(n_i) \prod_{p \mid \frac{n}{n}} \left(1 - \frac{1}{p^{2g}}\right)$$

$$\prod_{p \mid n} \left(1 - \frac{(-1)^{e_p-1}}{(p-1)^{e_p-1}}\right), \qquad (5.2.1)$$

where $e_p = \#\{i : 1 \le i \le k, p \nmid \frac{n}{n_i}\}$.

Proof. By Theorem 2.7.1, we have

$$|\mathrm{Epi}_S(\Gamma, \mathbb{Z}_n)| = \sum_{d \mid n} \mu\left(\frac{n}{d}\right) |\mathrm{Hom}_S(\Gamma, \mathbb{Z}_d)|, \qquad (5.2.2)$$

where $|\mathrm{Hom}_S(\Gamma, \mathbb{Z}_d)|$ is the number of surface-kernel homomor-phisms from Γ to $\mathbb{Z}_d$. It is easy to see that for every positive divisor d of n, we have $|\mathrm{Hom}_S(\Gamma, \mathbb{Z}_d)| = d^{2g}N_d$, where N_d is the number of solutions of the restricted linear congruence $x_1 + \cdots + x_k \equiv 0$ (mod d), with $(x_i, d) = \frac{d}{n_i}$ ($1 \le i \le k$). Suppose that $\mathfrak{D} := \{d > 0 : d \mid n$ and $\mathfrak{n} \mid d\}$. Clearly, if $\mathfrak{D}$ is empty, then $|\mathrm{Hom}_S(\Gamma, \mathbb{Z}_d)| = 0$, for every divisor d of n, which then implies that $|\mathrm{Epi}_S(\Gamma, \mathbb{Z}_n)| = 0$, by (5.2.2). Let $\mathfrak{n} \nmid n$. Then, $\mathfrak{n} \nmid d$ for every divisor d of n. Thus, $\mathfrak{D}$ is empty which then implies that $|\mathrm{Epi}_S(\Gamma, \mathbb{Z}_n)| = 0$, by (5.2.2). Now, let $\mathfrak{n} \mid n$. Then, there exists at least one divisor d of n such that $\mathfrak{n} \mid d$. So, $\mathfrak{D}$ is non-empty. Now, for every $d \in \mathfrak{D}$, by Theorem 3.2.9, we have

$$N_d = \prod_{i=1}^{k} \varphi(n_i) \prod_{\substack{p \mid d \\ \mathfrak{m}_p \le r_p}} p^{\mathfrak{m}_p - r_p - 1} \left(1 - \frac{(-1)^{e_p-1}}{(p-1)^{e_p-1}}\right), \qquad (5.2.3)$$

where r_p is the exponent of p in the prime factorization of d, $\mathfrak{m}_p$ is the smallest $j \ge 1$ such that there is some i with $p^j \nmid \frac{d}{n_i}$, and $e_p =$

$\#\{i : 1 \leq i \leq k, p^{m_p} \nmid \frac{d}{n_i}\}$. On the other hand, by Theorem 3.2.6, we have

$$N_d = \frac{1}{d} \sum_{d' \mid d} \varphi(d') \prod_{i=1}^{k} c_{n_i}\left(\frac{d}{d'}\right), \qquad (5.2.4)$$

which, as was proved by Tóth [193, Prop. 9], equals

$$N_d = \frac{1}{d} \sum_{q=1}^{d} \prod_{i=1}^{k} c_{n_i}(q). \qquad (5.2.5)$$

Now, since the Ramanujan sum $c_n(m)$ is a periodic function of m with period n, it is easy to see (from the equivalent expressions (5.2.4) and (5.2.5)) that the value of N_d will remain the same if we replace d with $\mathfrak{n}$ in (5.2.3). Consequently, we obtain the following explicit formula for the number of surface-kernel homomorphisms from Γ to $\mathbb{Z}_d$:

$$|\text{Hom}_S(\Gamma, \mathbb{Z}_d)| = d^{2g} \prod_{i=1}^{k} \varphi(n_i) \prod_{\substack{p \mid \mathfrak{n} \\ m_p \leq r_p}} p^{m_p - r_p - 1}\left(1 - \frac{(-1)^{e_p - 1}}{(p-1)^{e_p - 1}}\right),$$

where r_p is the exponent of p in the prime factorization of $\mathfrak{n}$, m_p is the smallest $j \geq 1$ such that there is some i with $p^j \nmid \frac{\mathfrak{n}}{n_i}$, and $e_p = \#\{i : 1 \leq i \leq k, p^{m_p} \nmid \frac{\mathfrak{n}}{n_i}\}$.

Note that since $\mathfrak{n} = \text{lcm}(n_1, \ldots, n_k)$, for every prime divisor p of $\mathfrak{n}$, we have $p \nmid \frac{\mathfrak{n}}{n_i}$ for at least one i. This means that $m_p = 1$ for every prime divisor p of $\mathfrak{n}$. Also, note that

$$\prod_{p \mid \mathfrak{n}} p^{r_p} = \mathfrak{n}.$$

Therefore, we get

$$|\text{Hom}_S(\Gamma, \mathbb{Z}_d)| = \frac{d^{2g}}{n} \prod_{i=1}^{k} \varphi(n_i) \prod_{p \mid n} \left(1 - \frac{(-1)^{e_p - 1}}{(p-1)^{e_p - 1}}\right),$$

where $e_p = \#\{i : 1 \le i \le k, p \nmid \frac{n}{n_i}\}$.

Now, using (5.2.2), letting $d = vn$, and then using Lemma 2.1.3, we obtain

$$|\text{Epi}_S(\Gamma, \mathbb{Z}_n)| =$$

$$\sum_{n \mid d \mid n} \mu\left(\frac{n}{d}\right) \frac{d^{2g}}{n} \prod_{i=1}^{k} \varphi(n_i) \prod_{p \mid n} \left(1 - \frac{(-1)^{e_p - 1}}{(p-1)^{e_p - 1}}\right)$$

$$= \sum_{v \mid \frac{n}{n}} \mu\left(\frac{n/n}{v}\right) v^{2g} n^{2g-1} \prod_{i=1}^{k} \varphi(n_i) \prod_{p \mid n} \left(1 - \frac{(-1)^{e_p - 1}}{(p-1)^{e_p - 1}}\right)$$

$$= \frac{n^{2g}}{n} \prod_{i=1}^{k} \varphi(n_i) \prod_{p \mid \frac{n}{n}} \left(1 - \frac{1}{p^{2g}}\right) \prod_{p \mid n} \left(1 - \frac{(-1)^{e_p - 1}}{(p-1)^{e_p - 1}}\right),$$

where $e_p = \#\{i : 1 \le i \le k, p \nmid \frac{n}{n_i}\}$. □

Example 5.2.2:

(i) Let Γ be the co-compact Fuchsian group with signature $(1; 2, 3, 4)$. Find the number of surface-kernel epimorphisms from Γ to $\mathbb{Z}_{24}$.

Here, $n = \text{lcm}(2, 3, 4) = 12 = 2^2 \cdot 3$. Also, $2 \mid \frac{n}{n_1} = 6$, $2 \mid \frac{n}{n_2} = 4$, and $2 \nmid \frac{n}{n_3} = 3$. So, $e_2 = 1$. Therefore, by Theorem 5.2.1, we have

$$|\text{Epi}_S(\Gamma, \mathbb{Z}_{24})| = 0,$$

because

$$1 - \frac{(-1)^{e_2-1}}{(2-1)^{e_2-1}} = 1 - \frac{(-1)^{1-1}}{1^{1-1}} = 0.$$

Of course, this example also follows directly from Harvey's theorem (Theorem 2.6.1).

(ii) Let Γ be the co-compact Fuchsian group with signature $(2; 36, 500, 125, 9)$. Find the number of surface-kernel epimorphisms from Γ to $\mathbb{Z}_{9000}$.

Here, $n = \text{lcm}(36, 500, 125, 9) = \text{lcm}(2^2 \cdot 3^2, 2^2 \cdot 5^3, 5^3, 3^2) = 2^2 \cdot 3^2 \cdot 5^3 = 4500$. We have

$$2 \nmid \frac{n}{n_1} = 5^3, 2 \nmid \frac{n}{n_2} = 3^2, \quad 2 \mid \frac{n}{n_3} = 2^2 \cdot 3^2,$$

$$2 \mid \frac{n}{n_4} = 2^2 \cdot 5^3, \quad \text{so } e_2 = 2;$$

$$3 \nmid \frac{n}{n_1} = 5^3, \quad 3 \mid \frac{n}{n_2} = 3^2, \quad 3 \mid \frac{n}{n_3} = 2^2 \cdot 3^2,$$

$$3 \nmid \frac{n}{n_4} = 2^2 \cdot 5^3, \quad \text{so } e_3 = 2;$$

$$5 \mid \frac{n}{n_1} = 5^3, \quad 5 \nmid \frac{n}{n_2} = 3^2, \quad 5 \nmid \frac{n}{n_3} = 2^2 \cdot 3^2,$$

$$5 \mid \frac{n}{n_4} = 2^2 \cdot 5^3, \quad \text{so } e_5 = 2.$$

Now,

$$\prod_{p \mid 4500} \left(1 - \frac{(-1)^{e_p-1}}{(p-1)^{e_p-1}}\right)$$

$$= \left(1 - \frac{(-1)^{2-1}}{(2-1)^{2-1}}\right)$$

$$\times \left(1 - \frac{(-1)^{2-1}}{(3-1)^{2-1}}\right)\left(1 - \frac{(-1)^{2-1}}{(5-1)^{2-1}}\right) = \frac{15}{4}.$$

Therefore, by Theorem 5.2.1, we have

$$|\text{Epi}_S(\Gamma, \mathbb{Z}_{9000})|$$

$$= \frac{9000^4}{4500} \varphi\left(2^2 \cdot 3^2\right) \varphi\left(2^2 \cdot 5^3\right) \varphi\left(5^3\right) \varphi\left(3^2\right) \left(1 - \frac{1}{2^4}\right)$$

$$\times \frac{15}{4} = 7,381,125 \cdot 10^{12}.$$

(iii) Let Γ be the co-compact Fuchsian group with signature $(0; 36, 500, 125, 9)$. Find the number of surface-kernel epimorphisms from Γ to $\mathbb{Z}_{9000}$.

Here, since $g = 0$,

$$\prod_{p \mid \frac{n}{\mathfrak{n}}} \left(1 - \frac{1}{p^{2g}}\right) = \prod_{p \mid 2} \left(1 - \frac{1}{p^0}\right) = 0.$$

Therefore, by Theorem 5.2.1, we have

$$|\text{Epi}_S(\Gamma, \mathbb{Z}_{9000})| = 0.$$

Of course, this example also follows directly from Harvey's theorem.

Remark 5.2.3. *In the proof of Theorem 5.2.1, we use only a special case of Theorem 3.2.9 where $a_i = 1$ $(1 \leq i \leq k)$ and $b = 0$. But, there may be other generalizations/variants of these or other groups so that for counting the number of surface-kernel epimorphisms (or other relevant problems), we have to use the 'full power' of Theorem 3.2.9.*

Remark 5.2.4. *In order to get explicit values for $|\text{Epi}_S(\Gamma, \mathbb{Z}_n)|$ from Theorem 5.2.1, we only need to find the prime factorization of n, of $\mathfrak{n}$, and of the periods $n_1, \ldots, n_k$. Then, we can easily compute e_p, $\varphi(n_i)$,* *etc. In fact, even for Harvey's theorem (Theorem 2.6.1) we need to find these prime factorizations! So, Theorem 5.2.1 has roughly the same computational cost as Harvey's theorem.*

Clearly, for a co-compact Fuchsian group with all periods equal to each other, we have $e_p = \#\{i : 1 \le i \le k, p \nmid \frac{\mathfrak{n}}{n_i}\} = k$, for every prime divisor p of $\mathfrak{n}$. Therefore, we get the following simpler formula from Theorem 5.2.1.

Corollary 5.2.5. *Let Γ be a co-compact Fuchsian group with signature $(g; n_1, \ldots, n_k)$, where $n_1 = \cdots = n_k = \mathfrak{n}$. If $\mathfrak{n} \nmid n$, then there is no surface-kernel epimorphism from Γ to $\mathbb{Z}_n$. Otherwise, the number of surface-kernel epimorphisms from Γ to $\mathbb{Z}_n$ is*

$$|\mathrm{Epi}_S(\Gamma, \mathbb{Z}_n)| = \frac{n^{2g}\varphi(\mathfrak{n})^k}{\mathfrak{n}} \prod_{p \mid \frac{n}{\mathfrak{n}}} \left(1 - \frac{1}{p^{2g}}\right) \prod_{p \mid \mathfrak{n}} \left(1 - \frac{(-1)^{k-1}}{(p-1)^{k-1}}\right).$$

$$(5.2.6)$$

Interestingly, using Theorem 5.2.1, we can obtain an 'equivalent' form of Harvey's theorem (Theorem 2.6.1). (See also [126].) Note that conditions (i) and (iii) in Corollary 5.2.6 are exactly the same as, respectively, conditions (ii) and (iv) in Harvey's theorem.

Corollary 5.2.6. *Let Γ be a co-compact Fuchsian group with signature $(g; n_1, \ldots, n_k)$, and let $\mathfrak{n} := \mathrm{lcm}(n_1, \ldots, n_k)$. There is a surface-kernel epimorphism from Γ to $\mathbb{Z}_n$ if and only if the following conditions are satisfied:*

(i) $\mathfrak{n} \mid n$, and if $g = 0$ then $\mathfrak{n} = n$;

(ii) $e_p > 1$ for every prime divisor p of $\mathfrak{n}$;

(iii) if $\mathfrak{n}$ is even then e_2 is also even.

Proof. The proof simply follows by using the first part of Theorem 5.2.1 and examining the conditions under which the factors of the products in (5.2.1) do not vanish. □

5.3 A PROBLEM

It is an interesting problem to develop these counting arguments for the classes of non-cyclic groups. Such results would be very important from several aspects; for example, they may lead to more extensions of Harvey's theorem and new proofs for the existing ones, and also may provide us new ways for dealing with the minimum genus and maximum order problems for these classes of groups. So, we pose the following question.

Problem 5.1. Give explicit formulas for the number of surface-kernel epimorphisms from a co-compact Fuchsian group to a non-cyclic group, say, Abelian, solvable, dihedral, etc.

CHAPTER 6

Alldiff Congruences, Graph Theoretic Method, and Beyond

6.1 INTRODUCTION

In Chapter 3, we studied the number of solutions of the linear congruence $a_1x_1 + \cdots + a_kx_k \equiv b \pmod{n}$, with the restrictions $(x_i, n) = t_i$ $(1 \le i \le k)$, where $a_1, t_1, \ldots, a_k, t_k, b, n$ $(n \ge 1)$ are arbitrary integers. Another restriction of potential interest is imposing the condition that all x_i are *distinct*. We call such congruences *alldiff congruences*. More formally, we call the linear congruence $a_1x_1 + \cdots + a_kx_k \equiv b \pmod{n}$ an *alldiff congruence* if all x_i are *distinct*. Unlike the gcd-restricted linear congruences, there seems to be very little published on alldiff congruences. Recently, Grynkiewicz et al. [75], using tools from additive combinatorics and group theory, proved necessary and sufficient conditions under which alldiff congruences have a solution; see also [2] and [75] for connections to zero-sum theory. So, it would be an interesting problem to give an explicit formula for the number of such solutions. Quite surprisingly, this problem was first considered, in a special case, by Schönemann [174] almost two centuries ago(!), but his result seems to have been overlooked. Schönemann [174] proved the following result.

Theorem 6.1.1. *Let p be a prime, $a_1, \ldots, a_k$ be arbitrary integers, and $\sum_{i=1}^{k} a_i \equiv 0 \pmod{p}$, but $\sum_{i \in I} a_i \not\equiv 0 \pmod{p}$ for all $\emptyset \neq I \subsetneq \{1, \ldots, k\}$. The number $N_p(k)$ of solutions $\langle x_1, \ldots, x_k \rangle \in \mathbb{Z}_p^k$ of the linear congruence $a_1 x_1 + \cdots + a_k x_k \equiv 0 \pmod{p}$, with all x_i distinct, is independent of the coefficients $a_1, \ldots, a_k$ and is equal to*

$$N_p(k) = (-1)^{k-1}(k-1)! (p-1) + (p-1) \cdots (p-k+1).$$

In the next section, we generalize Schönemann's theorem using Proposition 1.1.1 and a result on graph enumeration, namely, Theorem 2.8.2. This seems to be a rather uncommon method in the area; besides, our proof technique or its modifications may be useful for dealing with other cases of this problem (or even the general case) or other relevant problems. In Section 6.3, we consider unweighted alldiff congruences and, using properties of Ramanujan sums and of the discrete Fourier transform of arithmetic functions, give an explicit formula for the number of their solutions. In Section 6.4, we discuss applications/connections to several combinatorial problems. In the next chapter, we discuss applications of these results to the VT codes.

6.2 GRAPH THEORETIC METHOD

Our generalization of Schönemann's theorem is obtained via a graph theoretic method, which may be also of independent interest.

Theorem 6.2.1. *Let $a_1, \ldots, a_k, b, n$ ($n \geq 1$) be arbitrary integers, and $(\sum_{i \in I} a_i, n) = 1$ for all $\emptyset \neq I \subsetneq \{1, \ldots, k\}$. The number*

$N_n(b; a_1, \ldots, a_k)$ *of solutions* $\langle x_1, \ldots, x_k \rangle \in \mathbb{Z}_n^k$ *of the linear congruence* $a_1 x_1 + \cdots + a_k x_k \equiv b \pmod{n}$, *with all* x_i *distinct, is*

$$N_n(b; a_1, \ldots, a_k)$$

$$= \begin{cases} (-1)^k (k-1)! + (n-1)\cdots(n-k+1), \\ \quad \text{if } \left(\sum\limits_{i=1}^{k} a_i, n \right) \nmid b, \\[2em] (-1)^{k-1}(k-1)! \left(\left(\sum\limits_{i=1}^{k} a_i, n \right) - 1 \right) + (n-1)\cdots(n-k+1), \\ \quad \text{if } \left(\sum\limits_{i=1}^{k} a_i, n \right) \mid b. \end{cases}$$

Proof. Let $\langle x_1, \ldots, x_k \rangle \in \mathbb{Z}_n^k$ be a solution of the linear congruence $a_1 x_1 + \cdots + a_k x_k \equiv b \pmod{n}$. Note that our desired solutions are those for which none of the $\binom{k}{2}$ equalities $x_u = x_v$, $1 \leq u < v \leq k$, holds. Let $T_k = \{\{u, v\} : 1 \leq u < v \leq k\}$. By the inclusion-exclusion principle, the number of such solutions is

$$N_n(b; a_1, \ldots, a_k) = \sum_{e=0}^{\binom{k}{2}} (-1)^e \sum_{\substack{S \subseteq T_k \\ |S|=e}} N(S), \qquad (6.2.1)$$

where $N(S)$ is the number of solutions of the linear congruence with $x_\alpha = x_\beta$ for $\{\alpha, \beta\} \in S$.

Now, we need to calculate

$$\sum_{\substack{S \subseteq T_k \\ |S|=e}} N(S).$$

In order to calculate $N(S)$, we construct the graph $G(S)$ on vertices $1, \ldots, k$ and edge set S. In calculating $N(S)$, we note that all vertices i in a connected component of $G(S)$ correspond to the same x_i in the linear congruence (by the definition of $N(S)$), and so we can simplify the linear congruence by grouping the x_i that are equal to each other. This procedure eventually gives a new linear congruence in which the coefficients are of the form $\sum_{i \in I} a_i$, where $\emptyset \neq I \subseteq \{1, \ldots, k\}$, and the number of terms is equal to the number of connected components of $G(S)$. If $G(S)$ has $c > 1$ connected components, then since $(\sum_{i \in I} a_i, n) = 1$ for all $\emptyset \neq I \subsetneq \{1, \ldots, k\}$, by Proposition 1.1.1 we have $N(S) = n^{c-1}$. Also, if $G(S)$ is connected, that is, $c = 1$, then $N(S)$ is the number of solutions of the linear congruence $(\sum_{i=1}^{k} a_i)x \equiv b \pmod{n}$, and so by Proposition 1.1.1, $N(S)$, which we denote by A in this case, is equal to $(\sum_{i=1}^{k} a_i, n)$ if $(\sum_{i=1}^{k} a_i, n) \mid b$, and is equal to zero otherwise. Let $g(c, e, k)$ be the number of simple graphs with c connected components, e edges, and k vertices labeled $1, \ldots, k$, and let $g'(e, k)$ be the number of simple *connected* graphs with e edges and k labeled vertices. Now, recalling (6.2.1), we get

$$N_n(b; a_1, \ldots, a_k) = \sum_{e=0}^{\binom{k}{2}} (-1)^e \left(Ag'(e, k) + \sum_{c=2}^{k} n^{c-1} g(c, e, k) \right)$$

$$= A \sum_{e=0}^{\binom{k}{2}} (-1)^e g'(e, k) + \frac{1}{n} \sum_{e=0}^{\binom{k}{2}} \sum_{c=2}^{k} (-1)^e n^c g(c, e, k)$$

$$= (A - 1) \sum_{e=0}^{\binom{k}{2}} (-1)^e g'(e, k) + \frac{1}{n} \sum_{e=0}^{\binom{k}{2}} \sum_{c=1}^{k} (-1)^e n^c g(c, e, k).$$

Now, in order to evaluate the latter expression, we use the two formulas mentioned in Theorem 2.8.2. In fact, by Theorem 2.8.2, we have

$$\sum_{e,k} (-1)^e g'(e, k) \frac{z^k}{k!} = \log F(z, 0)$$

and

$$\sum_{c,e,k} (-1)^e n^c g(c, e, k) \frac{z^k}{k!} = F(z, 0)^n,$$

where F is the deformed exponential function. Note that $F(z, 0) = 1 + z$. Now, we have

$$\sum_{e=0}^{\binom{k}{2}} (-1)^e g'(e, k) = \text{the coefficient of } \frac{z^k}{k!} \text{ in } \log(1 + z), \text{ which is}$$

$$\text{equal to } \frac{k!(-1)^{k+1}}{k},$$

and

$$\sum_{e=0}^{\binom{k}{2}} \sum_{c=1}^{k} (-1)^e n^c g(c, e, k) = \text{the coefficient of } \frac{z^k}{k!} \text{ in } (1 + z)^n, \text{ which}$$

$$\text{is equal to } k!\binom{n}{k}.$$

Consequently, the number $N_n(b; a_1, \ldots, a_k)$ of solutions $\langle x_1, \ldots, x_k \rangle \in \mathbb{Z}_n^k$ of the linear congruence $a_1 x_1 + \cdots + a_k x_k \equiv b \pmod{n}$, with all x_i distinct, is

$$N_n(b; a_1, \ldots, a_k) = \frac{(A-1)k!(-1)^{k+1}}{k} + \frac{k!\binom{n}{k}}{n}$$

$$= \begin{cases} (-1)^k(k-1)! + (n-1)\cdots(n-k+1), \\ \quad \text{if } \left(\sum_{i=1}^{k} a_i, n\right) \nmid b, \\ (-1)^{k-1}(k-1)! \left(\left(\sum_{i=1}^{k} a_i, n\right) - 1\right) + (n-1)\cdots(n-k+1), \\ \quad \text{if } \left(\sum_{i=1}^{k} a_i, n\right) \mid b. \end{cases}$$

$\square$

Remark 6.2.2. *Note that in Schönemann's theorem b is zero and n is prime, but in Theorem 6.2.1 both b and n are arbitrary.*

6.3 UNWEIGHTED ALLDIFF CONGRUENCES

In this section, we obtain an explicit formula for the unweighted version of the problem. This also leads to interesting consequences.

Theorem 6.3.1. *Let n be a positive integer and $b \in \mathbb{Z}_n$. The number $N_n(k, b)$ of solutions $\langle x_1, \ldots, x_k \rangle \in \mathbb{Z}_n^k$ of the linear congruence $x_1 + \cdots + x_k \equiv b \pmod{n}$, with all x_i distinct, is*

$$N_n(k, b) = \frac{(-1)^k k!}{n} \sum_{d \mid (n, k)} (-1)^{\frac{k}{d}} c_d(b) \binom{\frac{n}{d}}{\frac{k}{d}}. \qquad (6.3.1)$$

Proof. It is well-known (see, e.g., [76, pp. 3–4]) that the number of partitions of b into exactly k *distinct* parts each taken from the given set A is the coefficient of $q^b z^k$ in

$$\prod_{j \in A} \left(1 + z q^j\right).$$

Now, take $A = \mathbb{Z}_n$ and $q = e^{2\pi i m/n}$, where m is a non-negative integer. Then, the number $P_n(k, b)$ of partitions of b into exactly k *distinct* parts each taken from $\mathbb{Z}_n$ (that is, the number of solutions of our linear congruence, with all x_i distinct, if order does not matter) is the coefficient of $e^{2\pi i b m/n} z^k$ in

$$\prod_{j=1}^{n} \left(1 + z e^{2\pi i j m/n}\right).$$

This in turn implies that

$$\sum_{b=1}^{n} P_n(k, b) e^{2\pi i b m/n} = \text{the coefficient of } z^k \text{ in } \prod_{j=1}^{n} \left(1 + z e^{2\pi i j m/n}\right).$$

Let $e(x) = \exp(2\pi i x)$. Note that $N_n(k, b) = k! P_n(k, b)$. Now, using Corollary 2.2.3, we get

$$\sum_{b=1}^{n} N_n(k, b) e\left(\frac{bm}{n}\right) = (-1)^{k + \frac{kd}{n}} k! \binom{d}{\frac{kd}{n}},$$

where $d = (m, n)$. Now, by (2.3.1) and (2.3.2), we obtain

$$N_n(k, b) = \frac{(-1)^k k!}{n} \sum_{m=1}^{n} (-1)^{\frac{kd}{n}} e\left(\frac{-bm}{n}\right) \binom{d}{\frac{kd}{n}}$$

$$= \frac{(-1)^k k!}{n} \sum_{d \mid n} \sum_{\substack{m=1 \\ (m, n)=d}}^{n} (-1)^{\frac{kd}{n}} e\left(\frac{-bm}{n}\right) \binom{d}{\frac{kd}{n}}$$

$$\overset{m'=m/d}{=} \frac{(-1)^k k!}{n} \sum_{d \mid n} \sum_{\substack{m'=1 \\ (m', n/d)=1}}^{n/d} (-1)^{\frac{kd}{n}} e\left(\frac{-bm'}{n/d}\right) \binom{d}{\frac{kd}{n}}$$

$$= \frac{(-1)^k k!}{n} \sum_{d \mid n} (-1)^{\frac{kd}{n}} c_{n/d}(-b) \binom{d}{\frac{kd}{n}}$$

$$= \frac{(-1)^k k!}{n} \sum_{d \mid n} (-1)^{\frac{kd}{n}} c_{n/d}(b) \binom{d}{\frac{kd}{n}}$$

$$= \frac{(-1)^k k!}{n} \sum_{d \mid n} (-1)^{\frac{k}{d}} c_d(b) \binom{\frac{n}{d}}{\frac{k}{d}}$$

$$= \frac{(-1)^k k!}{n} \sum_{d \mid (n, k)} (-1)^{\frac{k}{d}} c_d(b) \binom{\frac{n}{d}}{\frac{k}{d}}.$$

$\square$

Corollary 6.3.2. *If n or k is odd, then from (6.3.1) we obtain the following important special cases of the function $P_n(k, b) =$*

$\frac{1}{k!}N_n(k,b)$:

$$P_n(k,0) = \frac{1}{n} \sum_{d \mid (n,k)} \varphi(d) \binom{\frac{n}{d}}{\frac{k}{d}}, \qquad (6.3.2)$$

$$P_n(k,1) = \frac{1}{n} \sum_{d \mid (n,k)} \mu(d) \binom{\frac{n}{d}}{\frac{k}{d}}. \qquad (6.3.3)$$

Corollary 6.3.3. *If $(n,k) = 1$, then (6.3.1) is independent of b and simplifies as*

$$N_n(k) = \frac{k!}{n} \binom{n}{k}.$$

(Of course, this can also be proved directly.) If in addition we have $n = 2k + 1$, then

$$P_n(k) = \frac{1}{k!}N_n(k) = \frac{1}{2k+1} \binom{2k+1}{k} = \frac{1}{k+1} \binom{2k}{k},$$

which is the Catalan number.

Remark 6.3.4. *Using (2.1.8), it is easy to see that (6.3.1) also works when $k = 0$.*

Now, we introduce the important function $T_n(b)$, which is the sum of $P_n(k, b)$ over k. There are several interpretations for the function $T_n(b)$; for example, $T_n(b)$ can be interpreted as the number of subsets of the set $\{1, 2, \ldots, n\}$ that sum to b modulo n.

Corollary 6.3.5. *Let $T_n(b) := \sum_{k=0}^{n} \frac{1}{k!}N_n(k, b) = \sum_{k=0}^{n} P_n(k, b)$. Then, we have*

$$T_n(b) = \frac{1}{n} \sum_{\substack{d \mid n \\ d \text{ odd}}} c_d(b) 2^{\frac{n}{d}}. \qquad (6.3.4)$$

Proof. We have

$$T_n(b) = \sum_{k=0}^{n} \frac{(-1)^k}{n} \sum_{d \mid (n, k)} (-1)^{\frac{k}{d}} \binom{\frac{n}{d}}{\frac{k}{d}} c_d(b)$$

$$= \frac{1}{n} \sum_{\substack{d \mid n}} c_d(b) \sum_{\substack{k=0 \\ d \mid k}}^{n} (-1)^{k+\frac{k}{d}} \binom{\frac{n}{d}}{\frac{k}{d}}$$

$$= \frac{1}{n} \sum_{\substack{d \mid n \\ d \text{ odd}}} c_d(b) \sum_{\substack{k=0 \\ d \mid k}}^{n} (-1)^{k+\frac{k}{d}} \binom{\frac{n}{d}}{\frac{k}{d}}$$

$$+ \frac{1}{n} \sum_{\substack{d \mid n \\ d \text{ even}}} c_d(b) \sum_{\substack{k=0 \\ d \mid k}}^{n} (-1)^{k+\frac{k}{d}} \binom{\frac{n}{d}}{\frac{k}{d}}$$

$$= \frac{1}{n} \sum_{\substack{d \mid n \\ d \text{ odd}}} c_d(b) 2^{\frac{n}{d}}.$$

Note that in the last equality we have used the fact that if $d \mid n$ and d is even, then

$$\sum_{\substack{k=0 \\ d \mid k}}^{n} (-1)^{k+\frac{k}{d}} \binom{\frac{n}{d}}{\frac{k}{d}} = \sum_{\substack{k=0 \\ d \mid k}}^{n} (-1)^{\frac{k}{d}} \binom{\frac{n}{d}}{\frac{k}{d}} = 0.$$

□

What is the number of subsets of the set $\{1, 2, \ldots, n-1\}$ that sum to b modulo n? Using Corollary 6.3.5, we can obtain an explicit formula for the number of such subsets (see also [133]).

Corollary 6.3.6. *The number $T'_n(b)$ of subsets of the set $\{1, 2, \ldots, n-1\}$ that sum to b modulo n is*

$$T'_n(b) = \frac{1}{2} T_n(b) = \frac{1}{2n} \sum_{\substack{d \mid n \\ d \text{ odd}}} c_d(b) 2^{\frac{n}{d}}. \tag{6.3.5}$$

Proof. Let A be a subset of the set $\{1, 2, \ldots, n - 1\}$ that sums to b modulo n. Then, A and $A \cup \{n\}$ are both subsets of the set $\{1, 2, \ldots, n\}$, and both sum to b modulo n. Therefore, $T'_n(b) = \frac{1}{2}T_n(b)$. ☐

6.4 MORE APPLICATIONS AND CONNECTIONS

Interestingly, some special cases of the functions $P_n(k, b)$, $N_n(k, b)$, $T_n(b)$, and $T'_n(b)$ studied in this chapter have appeared in a wide range of combinatorial problems, sometimes in seemingly unrelated contexts. Here, we briefly mention some of these applications and connections.

6.4.1 Ordered Partitions Acted upon by Cyclic Permutations

Consider the set of all ordered partitions of a positive integer n into k parts acted upon by the cyclic permutation $(12 \ldots k)$. Razen et al. [158] obtained explicit formulas for the cardinality of the resulting family of orbits and for the number of orbits in this family having exactly k elements. These formulas coincide with the expressions for $P_n(k, 0)$ and $P_n(k, 1)$, respectively, when n or k is odd (see Corollary 6.3.2). Razen et al. [158] also discussed an application in coding theory in finding the complete weight enumerator of a code generated by a circulant matrix.

6.4.2 Permutations with Given Cycle Structure and Descent Set

Gessel and Reutenauer [68] counted permutations in the symmetric group S_n with a given cycle structure and descent set. One of their results gives an explicit formula for the number of n-cycles with descent set $\{k\}$, which coincides with the expression for $P_n(k, 1)$ when n or k is odd. Interestingly, the mapping introduced by Gessel and Reutenauer [68] has the *Burrows–Wheeler transformation* (BWT) as a special case. The BWT, introduced by Burrows and Wheeler [39], is a famous invertible data compression algorithm (see [46, 65]).

6.4.3 Fixed-Density Necklaces and Lyndon Words

If n or k is odd, then the expressions for $P_n(k,0)$ and $P_n(k,1)$ give, respectively, the number of fixed-density binary necklaces and fixed-density binary Lyndon words of length n and density k, as described by Gilbert and Riordan [70] and Ruskey and Sawada [165].

6.4.4 Necklace Polynomial

The function $T_n(b)$ is closely related to the polynomial

$$M(q,n) = \frac{1}{n} \sum_{d \mid n} \mu(d) q^{\frac{n}{d}},$$

which is called the *necklace polynomial* of degree n (it is easy to see that $M(q,n)$ is integer-valued for all $q \in \mathbb{Z}$). In fact, if n is odd then $M(2,n) = T_n(1)$. The necklace polynomials turn up in various contexts in combinatorics and algebra. For example, they appear as (see, e.g., [85, 112, 140, 185])

- the number of *aperiodic necklaces* (also called *Lyndon words*) of length n in an alphabet of size q (this justifies the name of 'necklace polynomial'); note that the number of *necklaces* of length n in an alphabet of size q is

$$\frac{1}{n} \sum_{d \mid n} \varphi(d) q^{\frac{n}{d}},$$

which coincides with the expression for $T_n(0)$ when $q = 2$ and n is odd);

- the number of monic irreducible polynomials of degree n over the finite field $\mathbb{F}_q$, where q is a prime power;

- the *Witt formula* in the context of free Lie algebras, which gives the number of basic commutators of degree n in the free Lie algebra on q generators;

- the exponent in the *cyclotomic identity*,

$$\frac{1}{1-qz} = \prod_{n=1}^{\infty} \left(\frac{1}{1-z^n}\right)^{M(q,\,n)},$$

which is a consequence of the Poincaré-Birkhoff-Witt Theorem (or PBW Theorem) on the structure of the universal enveloping algebras of Lie algebras (Metropolis and Rota [140] gave a bijective proof of this identity) and which is the main ingredient in the proof of the Witt formula.

6.4.5 Quasi-Necklace Polynomial

The function $T'_n(b)$ is also closely related to the polynomial

$$M'(q,n) = \frac{1}{2n} \sum_{d\,|\,n} \mu(d) q^{\frac{n}{d}},$$

which we call the *quasi-necklace polynomial* of degree n. In fact, if n is odd then $M'(2, n) = T'_n(1)$. The quasi-necklace polynomials also turn up in various contexts in combinatorics. For example, they appear as

- the number of transitive unimodal cyclic permutations obtained by Weiss and Rogers [209] (motivated by problems related to the structure of the set of periodic orbits of one-dimensional dynamical systems) using methods related to the work of Milnor and Thurston [143] (see also [192], which gives a generating function for the number of unimodal permutations with a given cycle structure);

- the number of periodic patterns of the tent map [10];

- the exponent in a problem related to casino shelf shuffling machines [56].

6.5 A PROBLEM

It would be an interesting problem to see if the techniques presented in this chapter can be modified so that it covers the problem in its full generality. So, we pose the following question.

Problem 6.1. Give an explicit formula for the number of solutions of alldiff congruences in the general case.

CHAPTER 7

Alldiff Congruences Meet VT Codes

7.1 INTRODUCTION

Based on the definition of the Varshamov–Tenengolts code $VT_b(n)$, we have $VT_0(5) = \{00000, 10001, 01010, 11100, 00111, 11011\}$, where we have shown vectors as strings. So, $|VT_0(5)| = 6$. What is the size of VT codes in general, that is, the number of codewords in the VT code $VT_b(n)$? Given a positive integer k, what is the number of codewords in $VT_b(n)$ with Hamming weight k? Ginzburg [71] considered the first question and proved an explicit formula for $|VT_b(n)|$ (in fact, he proved an explicit formula for the size of q-ary, rather than binary, VT codes, where q is an arbitrary positive integer).

In this chapter, we deal with these questions and obtain explicit formulas for them via a novel approach, namely, *connecting VT codes to alldiff congruences* studied in the previous chapter. This provides a general framework and gives new insight into all these problems, which might lead to further work.

7.2 MAIN RESULTS

Our first result in this section is an explicit formula for the size of VT codes. Of course, this result has been already discovered [71, 181, 186], but we derive it via a novel approach and as a consequence of our results on alldiff congruences from Chapter 6.

Theorem 7.2.1. *The size of the VT code $VT_b(n)$ is*

$$|VT_b(n)| = \frac{1}{2(n+1)} \sum_{\substack{d \,|\, n+1 \\ d \text{ odd}}} c_d(b) 2^{(n+1)/d}. \tag{7.2.1}$$

Proof. Let $\langle y_1, \ldots, y_n \rangle$ be a codeword in $VT_b(n)$. Note that $\sum_{i=1}^{n} i y_i$ is just the sum of some elements of the set $\{1, 2, \ldots, n\}$. Therefore, finding the number of codewords in $VT_b(n)$ boils down to finding the number of subsets of the set $\{1, 2, \ldots, n\}$ that sum to b modulo $n + 1$. The result now follows by a direct application of Corollary 6.3.6. $\qquad\square$

In some applications, for example, the one considered in this chapter, we also need to consider the case that all coordinates x_i are *positive* and *distinct*. Now, we obtain an explicit formula for the number of such solutions. Our main ingredient is Theorem 6.3.1, the explicit formula that we obtained in the previous chapter for the number of solutions of unweighted alldiff congruences.

Theorem 7.2.2. *Let n be a positive integer and $b \in \mathbb{Z}_n$. The number $N_n^{>0}(k, b)$ of solutions $\langle x_1, \ldots, x_k \rangle \in \mathbb{Z}_n^k$ of the linear congruence $x_1 + \cdots + x_k \equiv b \pmod{n}$, with all x_i positive and distinct modulo n, is*

$$N_n^{>0}(k, b) = \frac{(-1)^k k!}{n} \sum_{d \,|\, n} (-1)^{\lfloor \frac{k}{d} \rfloor} c_d(b) \binom{\frac{n}{d} - 1}{\lfloor \frac{k}{d} \rfloor}. \tag{7.2.2}$$

Proof. Clearly, $N_n^{>0}(k, b) = N_n(k, b) - N_n^0(k, b)$, where $N_n^0(k, b)$ denotes the number of solutions $\langle x_1, \ldots, x_k \rangle \in \mathbb{Z}_n^k$ with all x_i

distinct and one of the x_i being zero. Also, clearly, $N_n^0(k, b) = kN_n^{>0}(k - 1, b)$. Thus,

$$N_n(k, b) = N_n^{>0}(k, b) + kN_n^{>0}(k - 1, b). \qquad (7.2.3)$$

Now, using Theorem 6.3.1, we have

$$N_n(k, b) =$$

$$\frac{(-1)^k k!}{n} \sum_{d \mid (n, k)} (-1)^{\frac{k}{d}} c_d(b) \binom{\frac{n}{d}}{\frac{k}{d}}$$

$$= \frac{(-1)^k k!}{n} \sum_{d \mid (n, k)} (-1)^{\frac{k}{d}} c_d(b) \left(\binom{\frac{n}{d} - 1}{\frac{k}{d}} + \binom{\frac{n}{d} - 1}{\frac{k}{d} - 1} \right)$$

$$= \frac{(-1)^k k!}{n} \sum_{d \mid n} c_d(b) \left((-1)^{\frac{k}{d}} \binom{\frac{n}{d} - 1}{\frac{k}{d}} - (-1)^{\frac{k}{d} - 1} \binom{\frac{n}{d} - 1}{\frac{k}{d} - 1} \right)$$

$$= \frac{(-1)^k k!}{n} \sum_{d \mid n} c_d(b) \left((-1)^{\lfloor \frac{k}{d} \rfloor} \binom{\frac{n}{d} - 1}{\lfloor \frac{k}{d} \rfloor} - (-1)^{\lfloor \frac{k-1}{d} \rfloor} \binom{\frac{n}{d} - 1}{\lfloor \frac{k-1}{d} \rfloor} \right)$$

$$= \frac{(-1)^k k!}{n} \sum_{d \mid n} (-1)^{\lfloor \frac{k}{d} \rfloor} c_d(b) \binom{\frac{n}{d} - 1}{\lfloor \frac{k}{d} \rfloor}$$

$$+ k \frac{(-1)^{k-1} (k - 1)!}{n} \sum_{d \mid n} (-1)^{\lfloor \frac{k-1}{d} \rfloor} c_d(b) \binom{\frac{n}{d} - 1}{\lfloor \frac{k-1}{d} \rfloor}.$$

Note that in the fourth equality we have used the fact that $\lfloor \frac{k}{d} \rfloor = \lfloor \frac{k-1}{d} \rfloor + 1$ if $d \mid k$ and $\lfloor \frac{k}{d} \rfloor = \lfloor \frac{k-1}{d} \rfloor$ if $d \nmid k$. Now, recalling (7.2.3), we obtain the desired result. □

We believe that Theorem 7.2.2 is also a strong tool and might lead to interesting applications. For example, it immediately gives an explicit formula for the number of codewords in the VT code

$VT_b(n)$ with Hamming weight k, that is, the general term of the weight distribution of VT codes (see also [60] for a related result).

Theorem 7.2.3. *The number $|VT_b^{1,k}(n)|$ of codewords in the VT code $VT_b(n)$ with Hamming weight k is*

$$|VT_b^{1,k}(n)| = \frac{(-1)^k}{n+1} \sum_{d \mid n+1} (-1)^{\lfloor \frac{k}{d} \rfloor} c_d(b) \binom{\frac{n+1}{d} - 1}{\lfloor \frac{k}{d} \rfloor}. \qquad (7.2.4)$$

Proof. Let $\langle y_1, \ldots, y_n \rangle$ be a codeword in $VT_b(n)$ with Hamming weight k, that is, with exactly k 1s. Denote by x_j the position of the jth one. Note that $1 \leq j \leq k$ and $1 \leq x_1 < x_2 < \cdots < x_k \leq n$. Now, we have

$$\sum_{i=1}^{n} i y_i \equiv b \pmod{n+1} \iff x_1 + \cdots + x_k \equiv b \pmod{n+1}.$$

Therefore, finding the number of codewords in $VT_b(n)$ with Hamming weight k boils down to finding the number of solutions $\langle x_1, \ldots, x_k \rangle \in \mathbb{Z}_{n+1}^k$ of the linear congruence $x_1 + \cdots + x_k \equiv b \pmod{n+1}$, with all x_j positive and distinct and disregarding the order of the coordinates. The result now follows by a direct application of Theorem 7.2.2. □

CHAPTER 8

Binary Linear Congruence Code

8.1 INTRODUCTION

Deletions or insertions can occur in many systems; for example, they can occur in some communication and storage channels and in biological sequences. A deletion or insertion in a DNA sequence leads to a genetic mutation known as the frameshift mutation. Therefore, studying deletion/insertion correcting codes may lead to important insight into genetic processes and into many communication problems. Deletion correcting codes have been the subject of intense research for more than fifty years [139, 144, 181], with recent results settling long-standing open problems regarding constructions of multiple deletion correcting codes with low redundancy [34, 37]. Nevertheless, our understanding about these codes and channels with this type of error is still very limited, and many open problems in the area remain, especially when considering constructions of deletion correcting codes that satisfy additional constraints, such as weight or parity constraints. Examples include codes in the Damerau distance

[67], based on single deletion correcting codes with even weight, and Shifted Varshamov–Tenengolts codes [172] used for burst deletion correction. In such settings, one important question is to determine the weight enumerators of the component deletion correcting codes in order to estimate the size [47, 111] of the weight-constrained deletion correcting codes. The component deletion correcting code is frequently defined in terms of a linear congruence for which the number of solutions of some fixed weight determines the size of the constrained code.

In the following definition, we introduce a general class of codes that includes several well-known classes of deletion/insertion correcting codes as special cases. For example, the Helberg code, the Levenshtein code, the VT code, and most variants of these codes including most of those that have been recently used in studying DNA-based data storage systems are all special cases of our code. Then, using a number theoretic method, we give an explicit formula for the weight enumerator of our code, which in turn gives explicit formulas for the weight enumerators and for the sizes of the aforementioned codes (see also [47, 111] for some general upper bounds for the size of deletion correcting codes).

Definition 8.1.1. Let n, k be positive integers, $a_1, \ldots, a_k \in \mathbb{Z}$, and $b \in \mathbb{Z}_n$. We define the *Binary Linear Congruence Code* (BLCC) $\mathcal{C}$ as the set of all binary k-tuples $\langle c_1, \ldots, c_k \rangle$ such that

$$a_1 c_1 + \cdots + a_k c_k \equiv b \pmod{n}.$$

What can we say about the size or, more generally, about the weight enumerator of the Binary Linear Congruence Code $\mathcal{C}$? In the next section, we give an explicit formula for the weight enumerator of $\mathcal{C}$. Then, we derive explicit formulas for the weight enumerators and for the sizes of the aforementioned deletion correcting codes. We also obtain a formula for the size of the Shifted VT codes.

8.2 WEIGHT ENUMERATOR OF THE BINARY LINEAR CONGRUENCE CODE

Using a simple number theoretic argument, we give an explicit formula for the weight enumerator (and the size) of the Binary Linear Congruence Code C. Another result that automatically follows from our result is an explicit formula for the number of binary solutions of an *arbitrary* linear congruence, which, to the best of our knowledge, is the first result of its kind in the literature and may be of independent interest.

The following lemma is useful for proving our main result.

Lemma 8.2.1. *Let n, k be positive integers. For any k-tuple $\mathbf{m} = \langle m_1, \ldots, m_k \rangle \in \mathbb{C}^k$, we have*

$$\prod_{j=1}^{k} \left(1 + ze \left(\frac{m_j}{n} \right) \right) = \sum_{\mathbf{d} \in \{0,1\}^k} e \left(\frac{\mathbf{d} \cdot \mathbf{m}}{n} \right) z^{w(\mathbf{d})}. \qquad (8.2.1)$$

Proof. Expand the left-hand side of (8.2.1) and note that $e(x)e(y) = e(x + y)$. □

Now, we are ready to state and prove our main result.

Theorem 8.2.2. *Let n, k be positive integers, $a_1, \ldots, a_k \in \mathbb{Z}$, and $b \in \mathbb{Z}_n$. The weight enumerator of the BLCC C is*

$$W_C(z) = \frac{1}{n} \sum_{m=1}^{n} e \left(\frac{-bm}{n} \right) \prod_{j=1}^{k} \left(1 + ze \left(\frac{a_j m}{n} \right) \right). \qquad (8.2.2)$$

Proof. By Lemma 8.2.1, for any k-tuple $\mathbf{m} = \langle m_1, \ldots, m_k \rangle \in \mathbb{C}^k$, we have

$$\prod_{j=1}^{k} \left(1 + ze \left(\frac{m_j}{n} \right) \right) = \sum_{\mathbf{d} = \langle d_1, \ldots, d_k \rangle \in \{0,1\}^k} e \left(\frac{\mathbf{d} \cdot \mathbf{m}}{n} \right) z^{w(\mathbf{d})}.$$

•

Let $\mathbf{y} = \langle y_1, \ldots, y_k \rangle \in \mathbb{Z}_n^k$ be a solution of the linear congruence $a_1 x_1 + \cdots + a_k x_k \equiv b \pmod{n}$. Then, we have

$$
e\left(\frac{-(\mathbf{m} \cdot \mathbf{y})}{n}\right) \prod_{j=1}^{k} \left(1 + ze\left(\frac{m_j}{n}\right)\right)
$$

$$
= \sum_{\mathbf{d} = \langle d_1, \ldots, d_k \rangle \in \{0,1\}^k} e\left(\frac{\mathbf{d} \cdot \mathbf{m} - \mathbf{m} \cdot \mathbf{y}}{n}\right) z^{w(\mathbf{d})}.
$$

Let $\mathbf{a} = \langle a_1, \ldots, a_k \rangle$ and $M = \{\langle a_1 m, \ldots, a_k m \rangle : m = 1, \ldots, n\}$. Note that since $\mathbf{y} = \langle y_1, \ldots, y_k \rangle \in \mathbb{Z}_n^k$ is a solution of the linear congruence $a_1 x_1 + \cdots + a_k x_k \equiv b \pmod{n}$, we get $a_1 y_1 + \cdots + a_k y_k = \alpha n + b$, for some $\alpha \in \mathbb{Z}$. Similarly, $a_1 d_1 + \cdots + a_k d_k = \beta n + b'$, for some $\beta \in \mathbb{Z}$ and $b' \in \mathbb{Z}_n$.

Therefore,

$$
\sum_{\mathbf{m} \in M} e\left(\frac{-(\mathbf{m} \cdot \mathbf{y})}{n}\right) \prod_{j=1}^{k} \left(1 + ze\left(\frac{m_j}{n}\right)\right)
$$

$$
= \sum_{\mathbf{d} \in \{0,1\}^k} \left(\sum_{\mathbf{m} \in M} e\left(\frac{\mathbf{d} \cdot \mathbf{m} - \mathbf{m} \cdot \mathbf{y}}{n}\right)\right) z^{w(\mathbf{d})}.
$$

Thus,

$$
\sum_{m=1}^{n} e\left(\frac{-m(\mathbf{a} \cdot \mathbf{y})}{n}\right) \prod_{j=1}^{k} \left(1 + ze\left(\frac{a_j m}{n}\right)\right)
$$

$$
= \sum_{\mathbf{d} = \langle d_1, \ldots, d_k \rangle \in \{0,1\}^k} \left(\sum_{m=1}^{n} e\left(\frac{m(\mathbf{d} \cdot \mathbf{a} - \mathbf{a} \cdot \mathbf{y})}{n}\right)\right) z^{w(\mathbf{d})}
$$

$$\Rightarrow \sum_{m=1}^{n} e\left(\frac{-m(\alpha n + b)}{n}\right) \prod_{j=1}^{k}\left(1 + ze\left(\frac{a_j m}{n}\right)\right)$$

$$= \sum_{\mathbf{d}=\langle d_1,\ldots,d_k\rangle \in \{0,1\}^k}\left(\sum_{m=1}^{n} e\left(\frac{m((\beta - \alpha)n + b' - b)}{n}\right)\right) z^{w(\mathbf{d})}.$$

Thus,

$$\sum_{m=1}^{n} e\left(\frac{-bm}{n}\right) \prod_{j=1}^{k}\left(1 + ze\left(\frac{a_j m}{n}\right)\right)$$

$$= \sum_{\mathbf{d}=\langle d_1,\ldots,d_k\rangle \in \{0,1\}^k}\left(\sum_{m=1}^{n} e\left(\frac{m(b' - b)}{n}\right)\right) z^{w(\mathbf{d})}$$

$$= \sum_{\mathbf{d}=\langle d_1,\ldots,d_k\rangle \in \mathcal{C}}\left(\sum_{m=1}^{n} e\left(\frac{m(b' - b)}{n}\right)\right) z^{w(\mathbf{d})}$$

$$+ \sum_{\mathbf{d}=\langle d_1,\ldots,d_k\rangle \in \{0,1\}^k \setminus \mathcal{C}}\left(\sum_{m=1}^{n} e\left(\frac{m(b' - b)}{n}\right)\right) z^{w(\mathbf{d})}.$$

By Lemma 2.1.1,

$$\sum_{m=1}^{n} e\left(\frac{m(b' - b)}{n}\right) = \begin{cases} n, & \text{if } n \mid b' - b, \\ 0, & \text{if } n \nmid b' - b. \end{cases}$$

Note that if $\mathbf{d} = \langle d_1,\ldots,d_k\rangle \in \mathcal{C}$, then $b' = b$ (and so $n \mid b' - b$), and if $\mathbf{d} = \langle d_1,\ldots,d_k\rangle \in \{0,1\}^k \setminus \mathcal{C}$, then $b' \neq b$ (and so $n \nmid b' - b$ because $b', b \in \mathbb{Z}_n$). This implies that

$$\sum_{\mathbf{d}\in\mathcal{C}}\left(\sum_{m=1}^{n} e\left(\frac{m(b' - b)}{n}\right)\right) z^{w(\mathbf{d})} = n \sum_{\mathbf{d}\in\mathcal{C}} z^{w(\mathbf{d})}$$

and

$$\sum_{\mathbf{d}\in\{0,1\}^k\setminus\mathcal{C}} \left(\sum_{m=1}^{n} e\left(\frac{m(b'-b)}{n}\right)\right) z^{w(\mathbf{d})} = 0.$$

Consequently,

$$W_{\mathcal{C}}(z) = \sum_{\mathbf{c}\in\mathcal{C}} z^{w(\mathbf{c})} = \frac{1}{n}\sum_{m=1}^{n} e\left(\frac{-bm}{n}\right) \prod_{j=1}^{k}\left(1 + ze\left(\frac{a_j m}{n}\right)\right).$$

$\square$

Setting $z = 1$ in (8.2.2) gives the size of the BLCC $\mathcal{C}$. Equivalently, it gives an explicit formula for the number of binary solutions of an *arbitrary* linear congruence.

Corollary 8.2.3. *Let n, k be positive integers, $a_1, \ldots, a_k \in \mathbb{Z}$, and $b \in \mathbb{Z}_n$. The number of solutions of the linear congruence $a_1 x_1 + \cdots + a_k x_k \equiv b \pmod{n}$ in $\mathbb{Z}_2^k$ is*

$$W_{\mathcal{C}}(1) = \frac{2^k}{n}\sum_{m=1}^{n} e\left(\frac{\eta m}{n}\right) \prod_{j=1}^{k}\cos\left(\frac{\pi a_j m}{n}\right) \geq 0, \qquad (8.2.3)$$

where $\eta = -b + \frac{1}{2}\sum_{j=1}^{k} a_j$. This implies that

$$W_{\mathcal{C}}(1) \leq \frac{2^k}{n}\sum_{m=1}^{n}\prod_{j=1}^{k}\left|\cos\left(\frac{\pi a_j m}{n}\right)\right|. \qquad (8.2.4)$$

Proof. We have

$$W_{\mathcal{C}}(1) = \frac{1}{n}\sum_{m=1}^{n} e\left(\frac{-bm}{n}\right) \prod_{j=1}^{k}\left(1 + e\left(\frac{a_j m}{n}\right)\right)$$

$$= \frac{1}{n}\sum_{m=1}^{n} e\left(\frac{-bm}{n}\right) \prod_{j=1}^{k} e\left(\frac{a_j m}{2n}\right) \prod_{j=1}^{k} \left(e\left(\frac{-a_j m}{2n}\right) + e\left(\frac{a_j m}{2n}\right)\right)$$

$$= \frac{1}{n}\sum_{m=1}^{n} e\left(\frac{-bm}{n}\right) e\left(\frac{m}{2n}\sum_{j=1}^{k} a_j\right) \prod_{j=1}^{k} 2\cos\left(\frac{\pi a_j m}{n}\right)$$

$$= \frac{2^k}{n}\sum_{m=1}^{n} e\left(\frac{\eta m}{n}\right) \prod_{j=1}^{k} \cos\left(\frac{\pi a_j m}{n}\right),$$

where $\eta = -b + \frac{1}{2}\sum_{j=1}^{k} a_j$. Consequently, we have

$$W_{\mathcal{C}}(1) \le \frac{2^k}{n}\sum_{m=1}^{n}\prod_{j=1}^{k} \left|\cos\left(\frac{\pi a_j m}{n}\right)\right|.$$

□

Remark 8.2.4. *Recently, Gabrys et al. [67] proposed several variants of the Levenshtein code that are all special cases of our BLCC $\mathcal{C}$. Theorem 8.2.2 hence provides explicit formulas for the weight enumerators of such codes.*

8.3 WEIGHT ENUMERATORS OF THE AFOREMENTIONED CODES

Using Theorem 8.2.2, we now describe explicit formulas for the weight enumerators (and the sizes) of the Helberg code, the Levenshtein code, and the VT code. Note that the same approach may be used to derive the weight enumerators of most variants of these codes since they are special cases of Binary Linear Congruence Codes $\mathcal{C}$. In addition, we derive a formula for the size of the Shifted VT code.

The Helberg code has the same structure as the BLCC $\mathcal{C}$ but with some additional restrictions on the coefficients and the modulus. So, Theorem 8.2.2 immediately gives the following result.

Theorem 8.3.1. *The weight enumerator of the Helberg code*
$H_b(k, s)$ *is*

$$W_{H_b(k,s)}(z) = \frac{1}{n} \sum_{m=1}^{n} e\left(\frac{-bm}{n}\right) \prod_{j=1}^{k} \left(1 + ze\left(\frac{v_j m}{n}\right)\right). \quad (8.3.1)$$

As the coefficients in the Helberg code are a modified version of
the Fibonacci numbers, it may be possible to connect trigonometric sums as used in Corollary 8.2.3 with the Fibonacci and Lucas
numbers [31], and hence simplify (8.3.1).

Corollary 8.3.2. *The size of the Helberg code* $H_b(k, s)$ *equals*

$$W_{H_b(k,s)}(1) = \frac{2^k}{n} \sum_{m=1}^{n} e\left(\frac{\eta m}{n}\right) \prod_{j=1}^{k} \cos\left(\frac{\pi v_j m}{n}\right), \quad (8.3.2)$$

where $\eta = -b + \frac{1}{2} \sum_{j=1}^{k} v_j$. *This implies that*

$$W_{H_b(k,s)}(1) \le \frac{2^k}{n} \sum_{m=1}^{n} \prod_{j=1}^{k} \left|\cos\left(\frac{\pi v_j m}{n}\right)\right|. \quad (8.3.3)$$

Theorem 8.2.2 also allows for deriving an explicit formula for
the weight enumerator of the Levenshtein code.

Theorem 8.3.3. *The weight enumerator of the Levenshtein code*
$L_b(k, n)$ *is*

$$W_{L_b(k,n)}(z) = \frac{1}{n} \sum_{m=1}^{n} e\left(\frac{-bm}{n}\right) \prod_{j=1}^{k} \left(1 + ze\left(\frac{jm}{n}\right)\right). \quad (8.3.4)$$

Corollary 8.3.4. *The size of the Levenshtein code $L_b(k, n)$ equals*

$$W_{L_b(k,n)}(1) = \frac{2^k}{n} \sum_{m=1}^{n} e\left(\frac{\eta m}{n}\right) \prod_{j=1}^{k} \cos\left(\frac{\pi j m}{n}\right), \quad (8.3.5)$$

where $\eta = -b + \frac{1}{4}k(k+1)$. This implies that

$$W_{L_b(k,n)}(1) \leq \frac{2^k}{n} \sum_{m=1}^{n} \prod_{j=1}^{k} \left|\cos\left(\frac{\pi j m}{n}\right)\right|. \quad (8.3.6)$$

Next, using Theorem 8.3.3, we give an explicit formula for the size of the Shifted VT code $SVT_{b,r}(k, n)$. Note that $SVT_{b,r}(k, n)$ represents the set of codewords in the Levenshtein code with even Hamming weight (when $r = 0$) or with odd Hamming weight (when $r = 1$).

Theorem 8.3.5. *If $r = 0$ then the size of the Shifted VT code $SVT_{b,0}(k, n)$ is*

$$|SVT_{b,0}(k, n)| = \frac{2^{k-1}}{n} \sum_{m=1}^{n} e\left(\frac{\eta m}{n}\right) \left(A + (-1)^k B\right), \quad (8.3.7)$$

and if $r = 1$ then the size of $SVT_{b,1}(k, n)$ is

$$|SVT_{b,1}(k, n)| = \frac{2^{k-1}}{n} \sum_{m=1}^{n} e\left(\frac{\eta m}{n}\right) \left(A + (-1)^{k+1} B\right), \quad (8.3.8)$$

where $\eta = -b + \frac{1}{4}k(k+1)$ and

$$A = \prod_{j=1}^{k} \cos\left(\frac{\pi j m}{n}\right) \text{ and } B = \prod_{j=1}^{k} i \sin\left(\frac{\pi j m}{n}\right).$$

Proof. To find the number of codewords in the Levenshtein code $L_b(k, n)$ with even Hamming weight (when $r = 0$) and with odd Hamming weight (when $r = 1$), we proceed as follows. If $r = 0$, then the size of $SVT_{b,0}(k, n)$ equals $\frac{1}{2}(W_{L_b(k,n)}(z) + W_{L_b(k,n)}(-z))|_{z=1}$, and if $r = 1$, the size of $SVT_{b,1}(k, n)$ equals $\frac{1}{2}(W_{L_b(k,n)}(z) - W_{L_b(k,n)}(-z))|_{z=1}$. Invoking Theorem 8.3.3 proves the claimed result. □

Using Theorem 8.2.2 we obtain the following formula for the weight enumerator of the VT codes. Due to the special structure of the coefficients in these congruences, our formula simplifies significantly.

Theorem 8.3.6. *The weight enumerator of the VT code $VT_b(n)$ is*

$$W_{VT_b(n)}(z) = \frac{1}{(z+1)(n+1)} \sum_{d \mid n+1} c_d(b)(1 - (-z)^d)^{\frac{n+1}{d}}. \quad (8.3.9)$$

Proof. Using Theorem 8.2.2, we get

$$W_{VT_b(n)}(z) = \frac{1}{n+1} \sum_{m=1}^{n+1} e\left(\frac{-bm}{n+1}\right) \prod_{j=1}^{n}\left(1 + ze\left(\frac{jm}{n+1}\right)\right).$$

Therefore,

$$(z+1)(n+1)W_{VT_b(n)}(z)$$

$$= \sum_{m=1}^{n+1} e\left(\frac{-bm}{n+1}\right) \prod_{j=1}^{n+1}\left(1 + ze\left(\frac{jm}{n+1}\right)\right)$$

$$= \sum_{\substack{d \mid n+1}} \sum_{\substack{m=1 \\ (m,n+1)=d}}^{n+1} e\left(\frac{-bm}{n+1}\right) \prod_{j=1}^{n+1}\left(1 + ze\left(\frac{jm}{n+1}\right)\right).$$

Now, using Lemma 2.2.1, we get

$$(z+1)(n+1)W_{VT_b(n)}(z)$$

$$= \sum_{d \mid n+1} \sum_{\substack{m=1 \\ (m,n+1)=d}}^{n+1} e\left(\frac{-bm}{n+1}\right)(1-(-z)^{\frac{n+1}{d}})^d$$

$$\overset{m'=m/d}{=} \sum_{d \mid n+1} \sum_{\substack{m'=1 \\ (m',(n+1)/d)=1}}^{(n+1)/d} e\left(\frac{-bm'}{(n+1)/d}\right)(1-(-z)^{\frac{n+1}{d}})^d$$

$$= \sum_{d \mid n+1} c_{(n+1)/d}(-b)(1-(-z)^{\frac{n+1}{d}})^d$$

$$= \sum_{d \mid n+1} c_{(n+1)/d}(b)(1-(-z)^{\frac{n+1}{d}})^d$$

$$= \sum_{d \mid n+1} c_d(b)(1-(-z)^d)^{\frac{n+1}{d}}.$$

$$\square$$

Corollary 8.3.7. *Setting $z = 1$ in (8.3.9), we re-derive Theorem 7.2.1 proved in the previous chapter for the size of the VT codes. Also, using the binomial theorem to find the coefficient of z^{k+1} in the sum of (8.3.9), we re-derive Theorem 7.2.3 proved in the previous chapter for the general term of the weight distribution of the VT codes.*

Remark 8.3.8. *Ginzburg [71] proved the following explicit formula for the size $|VT_{b,q}(n)|$ of the q-ary, rather than binary, Varshamov–Tenengolts code $VT_{b,q}(n)$, where q is an arbitrary positive integer:*

$$|VT_{b,q}(n)| = \frac{1}{q(n+1)} \sum_{\substack{d \mid n+1 \\ (d,q)=1}} c_d(b)q^{\frac{n+1}{d}}. \qquad (8.3.10)$$

This formula (in fact, a more complicated version of it) was later rediscovered by Stanley and Yoder [186].

Remark 8.3.9. *Since for all integers m and n with $n \geq 1$, one has $c_n(m) \leq \varphi(n)$, from (8.3.10) it is clear that the maximum number of codewords in the q-ary VT code $VT_{b,q}(n)$ is obtained for $b = 0$, that is,*

$$|VT_{0,q}(n)| = \frac{1}{q(n+1)} \sum_{\substack{d \mid n+1 \\ (d,q)=1}} \varphi(d)q^{\frac{n+1}{d}} \geq |VT_{b,q}(n)|,$$

for all b. This result was originally proved by Ginzburg [71].

Remark 8.3.10. *Setting $d = 1$ in (7.2.1) gives the bound*

$$|VT_0(n)| \geq \frac{2^n}{n+1}.$$

On the other hand, by a result of Levenshtein [121], the size of the largest single deletion correcting binary code of length n, where n is sufficiently large, is roughly $2^n/n$. Therefore, as it is well known, the VT codes $VT_0(n)$, for sufficiently large n, are close to optimal.

CHAPTER 9

Applications in Parallel Computing, AI, etc.

O NE OF THE MAIN APPLICATIONS of congruences is via the Chinese remainder theorem, which itself has many important applications in computing, coding theory, cryptography, signal processing, etc. (see, e.g., [57, 104, 206] and the references therein).

Congruences have also been used in many other areas. For example, congruences with the binary solutions studied in Chapter 8 have interesting applications in database security [99] and pseudo-telepathy games in quantum computing [33]. In this chapter, we discuss applications of congruences to parallel computing, artificial intelligence, computational biology, and the Subset-Sum Problem.

9.1 APPLICATION IN PARALLEL COMPUTING

Congruences have been used in designing pseudorandom number generators for dynamic-multithreading platforms [161, 119,

169, 187]. Dynamic multithreading (dthreading) is the integration of a runtime scheduler into a concurrency platform. Many concurrency platforms offer a *processor oblivious* model of computation, meaning the programmer does not have to manage the threads that a program will use, but rather the logical parallelism of the program, allowing the scheduler to handle the distribution of work across threads. This makes parallel programming much easier for the programmer, but introduces an element of non-determinism in runtime because the execution is dependent on how the scheduler distributes work; this poses a problem for debugging, since non-determinism precludes repeatability upon which programmers rely.

Knuth [104, p. 193] famously said, 'Look at the subroutine library of each computer installation in your organization, and replace the random number generators [RNGs] by good ones. Try to avoid being too shocked at what you find'. RNGs are crucial to randomized algorithms, which provide efficient solutions to a myriad of problems in computer science, such as Monte Carlo simulations and other important techniques. However, in dthreaded code, most RNGs usually fail in one of two ways. Typically, they either are non-deterministic or come with a high overhead. Take, for example, a serial RNG. If strands share the same RNG, then they are forced to wait for access to the RNG (since two strands cannot simultaneously access the same RNG). Also, if each strand has its own RNG, the output is non-deterministic because of the scheduler.

For this reason, Leiserson et al. [119] persuaded Intel to modify its C/C++ compiler, which provides the Cilk Plus concurrency platform, to include pedigrees [170], which enable efficient deterministic random number generation by uniquely identifying strands with low overhead. They use pedigrees to design a deterministic parallel random number generator (DPRNG) called DOTMIX, which hashes pedigrees, then mixes them into a random number. DOTMIX is a fast and reliable DPRNG that is comparable to the seminal Mersenne Twister (which is the default PRNG for many software systems) in terms of statistical quality [119]. Furthermore, since it is deterministic, it is useful for debugging purposes. The Cilk Plus concurrency platform was part of Intel's C/C++ compiler, but as of 2018 it is deprecated. The project is continued at MIT's Cilkhub [118] under the name *Open Cilk*, where it is now supported by the Tapir/LLVM compiler [171].

Leiserson et al. [119] proposed as 'an interesting topic for future research' the use of a faster hash function for DOTMIX. Very recently, Ritchie and Bibak [161] addressed this question and improved the speed of the algorithm roughly by a factor of two, without sacrificing any statistical quality. Specifically, they replaced the compression function used in DOTMIX (which is based on congruences; see Chapter 2) with a faster universal hash function family called Square Hash [64] (which is also based on congruences). Specifically, Ritchie and Bibak [161] constructed a new DPRNG, called SQUAREMIX, and showed that it is roughly twice as fast as DOTMIX. We also remark that it is possible to further improve the speed of the algorithm, but potentially at the expense of lowering the statistical quality [161].

DOTMIX has various industry applications. It was incorporated into Intel Cilk Plus and both the Intel and GNU C/C++ compilers [169]. DOTMIX has also been used in Intel's DPRNG library [169]. Steele et al. [187], inspired by DOTMIX, designed SPLITMIX, which has been included in Java JDK8 as the class `java.util.SplittableRandom`. As SPLITMIX also uses the DOTMIX compression function, it might be possible to also improve the SPLITMIX speed using SQUAREMIX. It would be interesting to investigate the impact of SQUAREMIX in these or other applications.

9.2 APPLICATION IN ARTIFICIAL INTELLIGENCE AND COMPUTATIONAL BIOLOGY

Congruences have made a fundamental impact on artificial intelligence and computational biology via the edit distance, but this connection seems to have been somewhat overlooked. Recall that Levenshtein [121], by giving an elegant decoding algorithm, showed that if $n \geq k + 1$ then the Levenshtein code $L_b(k, n)$ can correct a single deletion (and consequently, can correct a single insertion). Furthermore, Levenshtein [121] proved that if $n \geq 2k$ then the code $L_b(k, n)$ can correct either a single deletion/insertion error or a single substitution error. In this section, we discuss how the Levenshtein code (which is essentially the set of solutions of a specific congruence) has led to seminal applications.

Measuring the similarity between objects is an important problem with many applications in various areas. Much of natural language processing (NLP) is concerned with measuring how similar two strings are [97]. The most important measure of similarity of two strings (words) is the edit distance (also known as the Levenshtein distance; see [121]), which is defined as the minimum number of character deletions, insertions, or substitutions required to transform one string (word) into the other. (Note that the Hamming distance is a variant of the edit distance where only *substitutions* are allowed.) The edit distance and its generalizations/variants are widely used, for example, in approximate string matching and natural language processing [97, 131, 149] (e.g., spell checking/correction, speech recognition, spam filtering) and in computational biology [5, 63, 96] (e.g., to quantify the similarity of DNA sequences). Levenshtein introduced the edit distance (and observed that the edit distance function is a metric; in particular, it is symmetric and satisfies the triangle inequality) in his seminal paper [121], where he introduced a generalization of VT codes, namely, the Levenshtein code. The focus of Levenshtein's paper [121], as the title of his paper says, was actually on constructing the class of codes related to the edit distance, namely, codes capable of correcting deletions, insertions, and substitutions. Levenshtein [121] also observed that a code C can correct s deletions, insertions, or substitutions if and only if the edit distance between every two distinct codewords in C is greater than $2s$.

9.3 APPLICATION IN THE SUBSET-SUM PROBLEM

In this section, we discuss applications to the Subset-Sum Problem, which may lead to important results in various areas. Before this, let us mention an important problem. It would be interesting to see if the technique presented in Chapter 8 can be modified to give more efficient formulas for the size of the BLCC. So, we pose the following question.

Problem 9.1. Give an explicit and efficiently computable formula for the size of the Levenshtein code (general case) and more generally for the size of the Binary Linear Congruence Code. In other words, give an explicit and efficiently computable formula for the number of *binary* solutions of an *arbitrary* linear congruence.

Such results would be interesting from various aspects and also might have more applications/implications in information theory, computer science, and mathematics. There are also other motivations for studying this problem as discussed next.

The problems considered in this book can be considered as relevant to the Subset-Sum Problem (a special case of the Knapsack Problem) that is a fundamental problem in computer science with many applications in cryptography, computational complexity, balancing problems, scheduling, etc. (see, e.g., [100] and the references therein).

Definition 9.3.1 (The Subset-Sum Problem (SS).) Given integers $a_1, \ldots, a_k, b$, find a subset of the a_i (if one exists) that adds up to b, or, equivalently, find $x_i \in \{0, 1\}$ such that $\sum_{i=1}^{k} a_i x_i = b$. In the decision version of the problem, one is given the integers $a_1, \ldots, a_k, b$ and must decide whether there exist $x_i \in \{0, 1\}$ such that $\sum_{i=1}^{k} a_i x_i = b$.

The Subset-Sum Problem is one of Karp's 21 NP-complete problems [142] (it is in fact weakly NP-complete as there are pseudo-polynomial time algorithms for it; see [107]). Micciancio [141], motivated by applications to lattice-based cryptography, proposed a generalization of this problem to arbitrary rings and studied its average-case complexity.

Definition 9.3.2 (The Subset-Sum Problem for Arbitrary Rings.)
For any ring R and subset $S \subset R$, given elements $a_1, \ldots, a_k \in R$ and a target element $b \in R$, find $\langle x_1, \ldots, x_k \rangle \in S^k$ such that $\sum_{i=1}^{k} a_i \cdot x_i = b$, where all operations are performed in the ring. In the decision version of the problem, one is given the ring R, a subset $S \subset R$, elements $a_1, \ldots, a_k \in R$, and a target element $b \in R$ and must decide whether there exists $\langle x_1, \ldots, x_k \rangle \in S^k$ such that $\sum_{i=1}^{k} a_i \cdot x_i = b$.

When we are talking about a ring R and subset $S \subset R$, one of the most important and natural cases is when $R = \mathbb{Z}_n$ and $S = \mathbb{Z}_n^*$. What can we say about the decision version of the Subset-Sum Problem for Arbitrary Rings in this case? Interestingly, in Chapter 3 we automatically addressed this problem, even in a more general form, using our results on counting the number of solutions of restricted linear congruences. In fact, the number of solutions of the restricted linear congruences studied in Chapter 3 with $(x_i, n) = 1$ $(1 \leq i \leq k)$ is greater than zero if and only if the output of the decision version of the Subset-Sum Problem for Arbitrary Rings with $R = \mathbb{Z}_n$ and $S = \mathbb{Z}_n^*$ is 'yes'. Therefore, we have the following theorem.

Theorem 9.3.3. *The output of the decision version of the Subset-Sum Problem for Arbitrary Rings with $R = \mathbb{Z}_n$ and $S = \mathbb{Z}_n^*$ is 'yes' if and only if none of the cases of Corollary 3.2.11 holds.*

Also, as another natural case, taking $R = \mathbb{Z}_n$ and $S = \{0, 1\}$ leads to a generalization of the Subset-Sum Problem (where $n = +\infty$) known as the Modular Subset-Sum Problem.

Definition 9.3.4 (The Modular Subset-Sum Problem (SS(k,n)).)
Given integers $a_1, \ldots, a_k, b \in \mathbb{Z}_n$, find a subset of the a_i (if one

exists) that adds up to b modulo n, or, equivalently, find $x_i \in \{0, 1\}$ such that $\sum_{i=1}^{k} a_i x_i \equiv b \pmod{n}$. In the decision version of the problem, one is given the integers $a_1, \ldots, a_k, b \in \mathbb{Z}_n$ and must decide whether there exist $x_i \in \{0, 1\}$ such that $\sum_{i=1}^{k} a_i x_i \equiv b \pmod{n}$.

The $SS(k, n)$ has been studied extensively in cryptography [4, 90, 130] (mainly because it has simple operations, its hardness is exponential in some cases, and it appears to be secure against quantum attacks), computer science [12, 15, 107], and additive combinatorics [14, 18, 152, 190]. The dynamic programming algorithm of Bellman [17] solves $SS(k, n)$ in the pseudo-polynomial time $O(kn)$. Very recently, Koiliaris and Xu [107] improved this runtime to $O(\min\{\sqrt{k}n, n^{5/4}\} \log^2 n)$, which is currently the fastest deterministic pseudo-polynomial time algorithm for $SS(k, n)$.

Quite interestingly, $SS(k, n)$ is related to the problem considered in Chapter 8 and Problem 9.1 (on page 115) because the output of the decision version of $SS(k, n)$ is 'yes' if and only if the size of the BLCC (i.e., the number of binary solutions of linear congruences) is greater than zero. Therefore, applying Corollary 8.2.3, we have the next result.

Theorem 9.3.5. *The output of the decision version of $SS(k, n)$ is 'yes' if and only if*

$$\sum_{m=1}^{n} e\left(\frac{\eta m}{n}\right) \prod_{j=1}^{k} \cos\left(\frac{\pi a_j m}{n}\right) > 0, \qquad (9.3.1)$$

where $\eta = -b + \frac{1}{2} \sum_{j=1}^{k} a_j$.

Therefore, having an efficient formula (possibly a product formula like the one given in Chapter 3) for the size of the BLCC (Corollary 8.2.3) might lead to more efficient algorithms for $SS(k, n)$, and so might lead to many applications. This gives another motivation for studying Problem 9.1.

CHAPTER 10

Quadratic Congruences, Ramanujan Graphs, and the Golomb–Welch Conjecture

10.1 INTRODUCTION

The long-standing Golomb–Welch conjecture [72] states that there are no perfect Lee codes for spheres of radius greater than 1 and dimension greater than 2. Resolving this conjecture has been one of the main motivations for studying perfect and quasi-perfect Lee codes [89]. Very recently, Camarero and Martínez [40] showed that for every prime number $p > 5$ such that $p \equiv \pm 5 \pmod{12}$, the Cayley graph $\mathcal{G}_p = \mathrm{Cay}(\mathbb{Z}_p[i], S_2)$, where S_2 is the set of units of $\mathbb{Z}_p[i]$, induces a 2-quasi-perfect Lee code over $\mathbb{Z}_p^m$, where $m = 2\lfloor\frac{p}{4}\rfloor$. They also conjectured [40, Conj. 31] that the Cayley graph $\mathcal{G}_p = \text{Cay}(\mathbb{Z}_p[i], S_2)$ is a Ramanujan graph for every prime p such that $p \equiv 3 \pmod 4$. In this chapter, we solve this conjecture. Our main tools are Deligne's bound [54] for estimating a particular kind of trigonometric sum and Theorem 2.11.4, which gives the eigenvalues of Cayley graphs of finite Abelian groups. Our proof techniques utilize interactions between spectral graph theory, character theory, and coding theory, which may cultivate progress towards the solution of the Golomb–Welch conjecture.

10.2 QUADRATIC CONGRUENCES

In order to find the degree of the Cayley graph $\mathcal{G}_p = \text{Cay}(\mathbb{Z}_p[i], S_2)$, we need to evaluate the number of solutions of certain quadratic congruences. The problem of counting the number of solutions of quadratic congruences in several variables has been investigated, in a general form, by [194], where a general formula is proved. Specifically, Tóth [194] considered the quadratic congruence

$$a_1 x_1^2 + \cdots + a_k x_k^2 \equiv b \pmod n, \qquad (10.2.1)$$

where $b \in \mathbb{Z}$ and $\mathbf{a} = \langle a_1, \ldots, a_k \rangle \in \mathbb{Z}^k$, and proved an explicit formula (see Theorem 10.2.1) for the number $N_k(b, n, \mathbf{a})$ of solutions $\langle x_1, \ldots, x_k \rangle \in \mathbb{Z}_n^k$ of (10.2.1), when n is odd. The formula involves a special kind of trigonometric sum, namely, quadratic Gauss sums, which we now define. Let $e(x) = \exp(2\pi i x)$ be the complex exponential with period 1. For positive integers m and n with $(m, n) = 1$, the quantity

$$S(m, n) = \sum_{j=1}^{n} e\left(\frac{mj^2}{n}\right) \qquad (10.2.2)$$

is called a *quadratic Gauss sum*.

Theorem 10.2.1. *Let k, b, n be integers $(k, n \geq 1)$ and $\mathbf{a} = \langle a_1, \ldots, a_k \rangle \in \mathbb{Z}^k$. We have*

$$N_k(b, n, \mathbf{a}) = n^{k-1} \sum_{d \mid n} \frac{1}{d^k} \sum_{\substack{m=1 \\ (m,d)=1}}^{d} e\left(\frac{-bm}{d}\right) S(ma_1, d) \cdots$$

$$S(ma_k, d).$$

Note that the Gauss sum has the Ramanujan sum as a special case. Interestingly, when k is even, n is odd, and $(a_1 \cdots a_k, n) = 1$, the number of solutions can be expressed in terms of the Ramanujan sum (see [194] for a proof).

Theorem 10.2.2. *Let $k = 2m$, where m is a positive integer, b be an integer, n be an odd positive integer, $(a_1 \cdots a_k, n) = 1$, and $\mathbf{a} = \langle a_1, \ldots, a_k \rangle \in \mathbb{Z}^k$. We have*

$$N_k(b, n, \mathbf{a}) = n^{2m-1} \sum_{d \mid n} \frac{c_d(b)}{d^m} \left(\frac{(-1)^m a_1 \cdots a_{2m}}{d}\right).$$

Putting $k = 2$, $a_1 = a_2 = 1$, $b = 1$, and $n = p^r$ (a power of a prime) in Theorem 10.2.1 (or in Theorem 10.2.2 when p is an odd prime), the following special case is obtained (see [194]).

Lemma 10.2.3. *Let p be a prime and r be a positive integer. The number $N_2(1, p^r)$ of solutions of the quadratic congruence $x^2 + y^2 \equiv 1 \pmod{p^r}$ is*

$$N_2(1, p^r) = \begin{cases} p^r(1 - \frac{1}{p}), & \text{if } p \equiv 1 \pmod{4}, r \geq 1, \\ p^r(1 + \frac{1}{p}), & \text{if } p \equiv 3 \pmod{4}, r \geq 1, \\ 2, & \text{if } p = 2, r = 1, \\ 2^{r+1}, & \text{if } p = 2, r \geq 2. \end{cases}$$

10.3 PROOF OF THE CONJECTURE

In this section, we prove the conjecture proposed by Camarero and Martínez [40], by showing that the Cayley graph $\mathcal{G}_p = \mathrm{Cay}(\mathbb{Z}_p[i], S_2)$ is a $(p + 1)$-regular Ramanujan graph. First, we mention the proof ingredients.

If $\mathbb{F}$ and $\mathbb{E}$ are fields and $\mathbb{F} \subseteq \mathbb{E}$, then $\mathbb{E}$ is said to be an *extension* of $\mathbb{F}$, denoted by $\mathbb{E}\ /\ \mathbb{F}$. The *degree* of a field extension $\mathbb{E}\ /\ \mathbb{F}$, denoted by $[\mathbb{E}\ :\ \mathbb{F}]$, is the dimension of $\mathbb{E}$ as a vector space over $\mathbb{F}$. A field extension $\mathbb{E}\ /\ \mathbb{F}$ is called a *finite extension* if $[\mathbb{E}\ :\ \mathbb{F}] < \infty$. Let $\mathbb{F}_{q^n}$ be a finite extension field of the finite field $\mathbb{F}_q$. For $\alpha \in \mathbb{F}_{q^n}$, the *field norm* of α is defined by (see, e.g., [123, Def. 2.27])

$$N_{\mathbb{F}_{q^n}/\mathbb{F}_q}(\alpha) = \alpha^{(q^n-1)/(q-1)}. \tag{10.3.1}$$

The elements of $\mathbb{F}_{q^n}$ with field norm 1 are called the *units* of $\mathbb{F}_{q^n}$.

Lemma 10.3.1. *Let p be a prime such that $p \equiv 3 \pmod 4$. Then, for every $z \in \mathbb{Z}_p[i]$ the field norm of z coincides with the norm of z in the usual sense, that is, as the norm of a Gaussian integer modulo p.*

Proof. Let $z = a + bi \in \mathbb{Z}_p[i]$, where p is a prime and $p \equiv 3 \pmod 4$. Then, by (10.3.1), the field norm of z equals

$$\begin{aligned}
N_{\mathbb{Z}_p[i]/\mathbb{Z}_p}(a + bi) &= (a + bi)^{p+1} \\
&= (a + bi)(a + bi)^p \\
&= (a + bi)(a^p + b^p i^p) \\
&= a^{p+1} + ab^p i^p + ba^p i + b^{p+1} i^{p+1} \\
&\equiv a^2 + b^2 \pmod p,
\end{aligned}$$

where we have used Fermat's little theorem and also the binomial theorem for commutative rings of characteristic p (see, e.g., [123, Th. 1.46]), which says that in a commutative ring R of prime characteristic p, we have

$$(x + y)^{p^n} = x^{p^n} + y^{p^n},$$

for every $x, y \in R$ and every positive integer n. Note that the value $a^2 + b^2$ (mod p) is just the norm of z as a Gaussian integer modulo p. □

Deligne [54], using tools from algebraic geometry and cohomology, proved the following crucial bound.

Theorem 10.3.2. *Suppose that* $\mathbb{F}_{q^n}/\mathbb{F}_q$ *is the field extension of degree n of the finite field* $\mathbb{F}_q$, S_n *is the set of units of* $\mathbb{F}_{q^n}$, *and* χ *is a nontrivial character of the additive group of* $\mathbb{F}_{q^n}$. *Then,*

$$\left| \sum_{s \in S_n} \chi(s) \right| \leq n q^{\frac{n-1}{2}}.$$

Now, we are ready to prove our main result. This problem has been mentioned before [40, Conj. 31].

Theorem 10.3.3. *Let p be a prime, $p \equiv 3$ (mod 4), and S_2 be the set of units of* $\mathbb{Z}_p[i]$. *Then, the Cayley graph* $\mathcal{G}_p = \text{Cay}(\mathbb{Z}_p[i], S_2)$ *is a $(p + 1)$-regular Ramanujan graph.*

Proof. By Proposition 2.11.1, the ring $\mathbb{Z}_n[i]$ is a field if and only if n is a prime and $n \equiv 3$ (mod 4). Thus, for a prime p with $p \equiv 3$ (mod 4), we have $\mathbb{Z}_p[i] \cong \mathbb{F}_{p^2}$. Also, we know that for a prime p with $p \equiv 3$ (mod 4), $\mathbb{Z}_p[i]$ as an extension field of the finite field $\mathbb{F}_p$ has degree 2 (because $\{1, i\}$ can serve as a basis), that is, $[\mathbb{Z}_p[i] : \mathbb{F}_p] = 2$.

Note that S_2 is a symmetric subset of $\mathbb{Z}_p[i]$ and does not contain the identity element of $\mathbb{Z}_p[i]$. Since the Cayley graph $\mathcal{G}_p = \text{Cay}(\mathbb{Z}_p[i], S_2)$ is of order p^2, it has p^2 real eigenvalues. Also, by Lemma 10.2.3, the number of solutions of the quadratic congruence $x^2 + y^2 \equiv 1 \pmod{p}$ is $p + 1$, so $|S_2| = p + 1$, which means that $\mathcal{G}_p$ is $(p + 1)$-regular. By Theorem 2.11.4, the eigenvalues of $\mathcal{G}_p$ are determined by

$$\lambda_\chi = \sum_{s \in S_2} \chi(s),$$

where χ runs over all characters of $\mathbb{Z}_p[i]$; note that since $\mathbb{Z}_p[i]$, as an additive group, is a finite Abelian group, it has p^2 distinct characters. The eigenvalue corresponding to the trivial character χ_0 of $\mathbb{Z}_p[i]$ equals

$$\lambda_{\chi_0} = \sum_{s \in S_2} \chi_0(s) = \sum_{s \in S_2} 1 = |S_2| = p + 1.$$

Of course, as $\mathcal{G}_p$ is $(p + 1)$-regular, we already knew, by Proposition 2.11.3, that $p + 1$ is an eigenvalue of $\mathcal{G}_p$ (in fact, the largest one).

Note that since p is a prime and $p \equiv 3 \pmod{4}$, by Lemma 10.3.1, for every $z \in \mathbb{Z}_p[i]$ the field norm of z coincides with the norm of z as a Gaussian integer modulo p; thus, the 'field norm' (and so unit) in Theorem 10.3.2 is in fact the 'norm' (and so unit) that we already have. Now, by Theorem 10.3.2, the absolute values of the eigenvalues corresponding to the non-trivial characters $\chi \neq \chi_0$ of $\mathbb{Z}_p[i]$ satisfy the bound

$$|\lambda_\chi| = \left| \sum_{s \in S_2} \chi(s) \right| \leq 2\sqrt{p}.$$

Therefore, $\mathcal{G}_p$ is a $(p + 1)$-regular Ramanujan graph. We remark that since $\mathcal{G}_p$ is $(p + 1)$-regular and the eigenvalue $p + 1$ has multiplicity one, by Proposition 2.11.3, $\mathcal{G}_p$ is connected. This in turn implies that S_2 generates $\mathbb{Z}_p[i]$. □

Since by the previous argument, $-(p + 1)$ is not an eigenvalue of $\mathcal{G}_p$, by Proposition 2.11.3, we get the following corollary.

Corollary 10.3.4. *The Cayley graph* $\mathcal{G}_p = \text{Cay}(\mathbb{Z}_p[i], S_2)$ *is not bipartite. This implies that* $\mathcal{G}_p$ *has at least one odd cycle.*

10.4 A PROBLEM

It would be interesting to consider such problems also for the case that p is a prime with $p \equiv 1$ (mod 4). So, we pose the following question.

Problem 10.1. Let p be a prime, $p \equiv 1$ (mod 4), and S_2 be the set of units of $\mathbb{Z}_p[i]$. What can we say about the Cayley graph $\mathcal{G}_p = \text{Cay}(\mathbb{Z}_p[i], S_2)$? Can we prove that almost all such graphs are Ramanujan?

Probably the first step here would be to prove some character sum bound. Such a result would be very interesting from several aspects and most certainly would need deep tools from several areas of mathematics, in particular algebraic geometry and number theory.

Bibliography

1. Abdel-Ghaffar K. A. S., Paluncic F., Ferreira H. C., and Clarke W. A., On Helberg's generalization of the Levenshtein code for multiple deletion/insertion error correction, *IEEE Trans. Inform. Theory* 58 (2012), 1804–1808.
2. Adams D. and Ponomarenko V., Distinct solution to a linear congruence, *Involve* 3 (2010), 341–344.
3. Adhikari S. D., Chen Y. G., Friedlander J. B., Konyagin S. V., and Pappalardi F., Contributions to zero-sum problems, *Discrete Math.* 306 (2006), 1–10.
4. Ajtai M., Generating hard instances of lattice problems (extended abstract), In *Proceedings of the Twenty-Eighth Annual ACM Symposium on Theory of Computing (STOC 1996)*, ACM (1996), 99–108.
5. Al Aziz Md. M., Alhadidi D., and Mohammed N., Secure approximation of edit distance on genomic data, *BMC Med. Genomics* 10 (2017), Article 41.
6. Alder H. L., A generalization of the Euler φ-function, *Am. Math. Monthly* 65 (1958), 690–692.
7. Alomair B., Clark A., and Poovendran R., The power of primes: Security of authentication based on a universal hash-function family, *J. Math. Cryptol.* 4 (2010), 121–148.
8. Alomair B., Lazos L., and Poovendran R., Securing low-cost RFID systems: An unconditionally secure approach, *J. Comput. Secur.* 19 (2011), 229–257.
9. Alomair B. and Poovendran R., Information theoretically secure encryption with almost free authentication, *J. UCS* 15 (2009), 2937–2956.

10. Archer K. and Elizalde S., Cyclic permutations realized by signed shifts, *J. Combin.* 5 (2014), 1–30.

11. Ardila F., Castillo F., and Henley M., The arithmetic Tutte polynomials of the classical root systems, *Int. Math. Res. Not.* 2015 (2015), 3830–3877.

12. Axiotis K., Backurs A., Jin C., Tzamos C., and Wu H., Fast modular subset sum using linear sketching, In *Proceedings of the Thirtieth Annual ACM-SIAM Symposium on Discrete Algorithms (SODA 2019)*, SIAM (2019), 58–69.

13. Babai L., Spectra of Cayley graphs, *J. Combin. Theory Ser. B* 27 (1979), 180–189.

14. Balandraud E., Girard B., Griffiths S., and Hamidoune Y., Subset sums in abelian groups, *Eur. J. Combin.* 34 (2013), 1269–1286.

15. Bansal N., Garg S., Nederlof J., and Vyas N., Faster space-efficient algorithms for subset sum, k-sum, and related problems, *SIAM J. Comput.* 47 (2018), 1755–1777.

16. Bellare M. and Namprempre C., Authenticated encryption: Relations among notions and analysis of the generic composition paradigm, *Advances in Cryptology—ASIACRYPT 2000*, Lecture Notes in Computer Science 1976, Springer (2000), 531–545.

17. Bellman R., Notes on the theory of dynamic programming IV— Maximization over discrete sets, *Naval Res. Logist. Quart.* 3 (1956), 67–70.

18. Bibak K., Additive combinatorics with a view towards computer science and cryptography, In Borwein J. M., Shparlinski I. E., and Zudilin W. (eds.), *Number Theory and Related Fields: In Memory of Alf van der Poorten*, Springer Proceedings in Mathematics & Statistics 43, Springer (2013), 99–128.

19. Bibak K., Order-restricted linear congruences, *Discrete Math.* 343 (2020), 111690.

20. Bibak K., Kapron B. M., and Srinivasan V., The Cayley graphs associated with some quasi-perfect Lee codes are Ramanujan graphs, *IEEE Trans. Inform. Theory* 62 (2016a), 6355–6358.

21. Bibak K., Kapron B. M., and Srinivasan V., Counting surface-kernel epimorphisms from a co-compact Fuchsian group to a cyclic group with motivations from string theory and QFT, *Nuclear Phys. B* 910 (2016b), 712–723.

22. Bibak K., Kapron B. M., and Srinivasan V., MMH with arbitrary modulus is always almost-universal, *Inform. Process. Lett.* 116 (2016c), 481–483.

23. Bibak K., Kapron B. M., and Srinivasan V., On a restricted linear congruence, *Int. J. Number Theory* 12 (2016d), 2167–2171.

24. Bibak K., Kapron B. M., and Srinivasan V., Unweighted linear congruences with distinct coordinates and the Varshamov–Tenengolts codes, *Des. Codes Cryptogr.* 86 (2018), 1893–1904.

25. Bibak K., Kapron B. M., and Srinivasan V., A generalization of Schönemann's theorem via a graph theoretic method, *Discrete Math.* 342 (2019), 3057–3061.

26. Bibak K., Kapron B. M., Srinivasan V., Tauraso R., and Tóth L., Restricted linear congruences, *J. Number Theory* 171 (2017), 128–144.

27. Bibak K., Kapron B. M., Srinivasan V., and Tóth L., On a variant of multilinear modular hashing with applications to authentication and secrecy codes, In *Proceedings of the International Symposium on Information Theory and Its Applications—ISITA 2016*, Institute of Electronics, Information and Communication Engineers (2016), 320–324.

28. Bibak K., Kapron B. M., Srinivasan V., and Tóth L., On an almost-universal hash function family with applications to authentication and secrecy codes, *Int. J. Found. Comput. Sci.* 29 (2018), 357–375.

29. Bibak K. and Milenkovic O., Weight enumerators of some classes of deletion correcting codes, In *Proceedings of the 2018 IEEE International Symposium on Information Theory (ISIT 2018)*, IEEE Press (2018), 431–435.

30. Bibak K. and Milenkovic O., Explicit formulas for the weight enumerators of some classes of deletion correcting codes, *IEEE Trans. Commun.* 67 (2019), 1809–1816.

31. Bibak K. and Shirdareh Haghighi M. H., Some trigonometric identities involving Fibonacci and Lucas numbers, *J. Integer Seq.* 12 (2009), Article 09.8.4.

32. Black J., Halevi S., Krawczyk H., Krovetz T., and Rogaway P., UMAC: Fast and secure message authentication, In *Advances in Cryptology—CRYPTO 1999*, Lecture Notes in Computer Science 1666, Springer (1999), 216–233.

33. Boyer M., Extended GHZ n-player games with classical probability of winning tending to 0, arXiv:quant-ph/0408090 (2004).

34. Brakensiek J., Guruswami V., and Zbarsky S., Efficient low-redundancy codes for correcting multiple deletions, *IEEE Trans. Inform. Theory* 64 (2018), 3403–3410.

35. Brauer A., Lösung der Aufgabe 30, *Jber. Deutsch. Math.-Verein* 35 (1926), 92–94.

36. Bujalance E., Cirre F.-J., and Gromadzki G., A survey of research inspired by Harvey's theorem on cyclic groups of automorphisms, In *Geometry of Riemann Surfaces*, London Matematical Society Lecture Note Series 368, Cambridge University Press (2010), 15–37.

37. Bukh B., Guruswami V., and Håstad J., An improved bound on the fraction of correctable deletions, *IEEE Trans. Inform. Theory* 63 (2017), 93–103.

38. Burnside W., *Theory of Groups of Finite Order*, Dover Publications (1955).

39. Burrows M. and Wheeler D. J., A block-sorting lossless data compression algorithm, Technical Report 124, Digital Equipment Corporation, Palo Alto, California, USA (1994).

40. Camarero C. and Martínez C., Quasi-perfect Lee codes of radius 2 and arbitrarily large dimension, *IEEE Trans. Inform. Theory* 62 (2016), 1183–1192.

41. Carter J. L. and Wegman M. N., Universal classes of hash functions, *J. Comput. System Sci* 18 (1979), 143–154.

42. Cohen E., A class of arithmetical functions, *Proc. Natl. Acad. Sci. USA* 41 (1955a), 939–944.

43. Cohen E., An extension of Ramanujan's sums. II. Additive properties, *Duke Math. J.* 22 (1955b), 543–550.

44. Cohen E., Representations of even functions (mod *r*). III. Special topics, *Duke Math. J.* 26 (1959), 491–500.

45. Constantin S. D. and Rao T. R. N., On the theory of binary asymmetric error correcting codes, *Inform. Contr.* 40 (1979), 20–36.

46. Crochemore M., Désarménien J., and Perrin D., A note on the Burrows-Wheeler transformation, *Theoret. Comput. Sci.* 332 (2005), 567–572.

47. Cullina D. and Kiyavash N., An improvement to Levenshtein's upper bound on the cardinality of deletion correcting codes, *IEEE Trans. Inform. Theory* 60 (2014), 3862–3870.

48. Cullina D., Kiyavash N., and Kulkarni A. A., Restricted composition deletion correcting codes, *IEEE Trans. Inform. Theory* 62 (2016), 4819–4832.

49. Cullina D., Kulkarni A. A., and Kiyavash N., A coloring approach to constructing deletion correcting codes from constant weight subgraphs, In *2012 IEEE International Symposium on Information Theory Proceedings*, IEEE Press (2012), 513–517.

50. Cvetković D., Doob M., and Sachs H., *Spectra of Graphs: Theory and Applications*, 3rd ed, Johann Ambrosius Barth (1995).

51. Davidoff G., Sarnak P., and Valette A., *Elementary Number Theory, Group Theory and Ramanujan Graphs*, Cambridge University Press (2003).

52. Deaconescu M., Adding units mod *n*, *Elem. Math.* 55 (2000), 123–127.

53. Deaconescu M., On the equation $m - 1 = a\varphi(m)$, *Integers: Electron. J. Combin. Number Theory* 6 (A06) (2006).

54. Deligne P., *Cohomologie Étale, SGA* $4\frac{1}{2}$, Springer-Verlag (1977).

55. Delsarte Ph. and Piret Ph., Spectral enumerators for certain additive-error-correcting codes over integer alphabets, *Inform. Contr.* 48 (1981), 193–210.

56. Diaconis P., Fulman J., and Holmes S., Analysis of casino shelf shuffling machines, *Ann. Appl. Probab.* 23 (2013), 1692–1720.

57. Ding C., Pei D., and Salomaa A., *Chinese Remainder Theorem: Applications in Computing, Coding, Cryptography*, World Scientific (1996).

58. Dixon J. D., A finite analogue of the Goldbach problem, *Canad. Math. Bull.* 3 (1960), 121–126.

59. Dodis Y., Ostrovsky R., Reyzin L., and Smith A., Fuzzy extractors: How to generate strong keys from biometrics and other noisy data, *SIAM J. Comput.* 38 (2008), 97–139.

60. Dolecek L. and Anantharam V., Repetition error correcting sets: Explicit constructions and prefixing methods, *SIAM J. Discrete Math.* 23 (2010), 2120–2146.

61. Dresden G. and Dymàček W. M., Finding factors of factor rings over the Gaussian integers, *Am. Math. Monthly* 112 (2005), 602–611.

62. Droll A., A classification of Ramanujan unitary Cayley graphs, *Electron. J. Combin.* 17 (2010), Article N29.

63. Durbin R., Eddy S. R., Krogh A., and Mitchison G., *Biological Sequence Analysis: Probabilistic Models of Proteins and Nucleic Acids*, Cambridge University Press (1998).

64. Etzel M., Patel S., and Ramzan Z., SQUARE HASH: Fast message authenication via optimized universal hash functions, In *Advances in Cryptology—CRYPTO '99*, Lecture Notes in Computer Science 1666, Springer (1999), 234–251.

65. Ferragina P., Giancarlo R., Manzini G., and Sciortino M., Boosting textual compression in optimal linear time, *J. ACM* 52 (2005), 688–713.

66. Fowler C. F., Garcia S. R., and Karaali G., Ramanujan sums as supercharacters, *Ramanujan J.* 35 (2014), 205–241.

67. Gabrys R., Yaakobi E., and Milenkovic O., Codes in the Damerau distance for deletion and adjacent transposition correction, *IEEE Trans. Inform. Theory* 64 (2018), 2550–2570.

68. Gessel I. M. and Reutenauer C., Counting permutations with given cycle structure and descent set, *J. Combin. Theory Ser. A* 64 (1993), 189–215.

69. Gilbert E. N., MacWilliams F. J., and Sloane N. J. A., Codes which detect deception, *Bell Syst. Tech. J.* 53 (1974), 405–424.

70. Gilbert E. N. and Riordan J., Symmetry types of periodic sequences, *Illinois J. Math.* 5 (1961), 657–665.

71. Ginzburg B. D., A certain number-theoretic function which has an application in coding theory (in Russian), *Problemy Kibernet.* 19 (1967), 249–252.

72. Golomb S. W. and Welch L. R., Perfect codes in the Lee metric and the packing of polyominoes, *SIAM J. Appl. Math.* 18 (1970), 302–317.

73. Greenberg L., Conformal transformations of Riemann surfaces, *Am. J. Math.* 82 (1960), 749–760.

74. Grošek O. and Porubský Š., Coprime solutions to $ax \equiv b$ (mod n), *J. Math. Cryptol.* 7 (2013), 217–224.

75. Grynkiewicz D. J., Philipp A., and Ponomarenko V., Arithmetic-progression-weighted subsequence sums, *Israel J. Math.* 193 (2013), 359–398.

76. Gupta H., Partitions—A survey, *J. Res. Nat. Bur. Standards—B. Math. Sci.* 74B (1970), 1–29.

77. Hagiwara M., A short proof for the multi-deletion error correction property of Helberg codes, *IEICE Comm. Express* 5 (2016), 49–51.

78. Halevi S. and Krawczyk H., MMH: Software message authentication in the Gbit/second rates, In *Fast Software Encryption—FSE 1997*, Lecture Notes in Computer Science 1267, Springer (1997), 172–189.

79. Hall P., The Eulerian functions of a group, *Q. J. Math.* 7 (1936), 134–151.

80. Handschuh H. and Preneel B., Key-recovery attacks on universal hash function based MAC algorithms, *Advances in Cryptology—CRYPTO 2008*, Lecture Notes in Computer Science 5157, Springer (2008), 144–161.

81. Harvey W. J., Cyclic groups of automorphisms of a compact Riemann surface, *Q. J. Math.* 17 (1966), 86–97.

82. Håstad J., Impagliazzo R., Levin L. A., and Luby M., A pseudorandom generator from any one-way function, *SIAM J. Comput.* 28 (1999), 1364–1396.

83. Hayashi M., General nonasymptotic and asymptotic formulas in channel resolvability and identification capacity and their application to the wiretap channel, *IEEE Trans. Inf. Theory* 52 (2006), 1562–1575.

84. Hayashi M., Exponential decreasing rate of leaked information in universal random privacy amplification, *IEEE Trans. Inf. Theory* 57 (2011), 3989–4001.

85. Hazewinkel M., Witt vectors. Part 1, In Hazewinkel M. (ed.), *Handbook of Algebra*, vol. 6, Elsevier (2009), 319–472.

86. Helberg A. S. J. and Ferreira H. C., On multiple insertion/deletion correcting codes, *IEEE Trans. Inform. Theory* 48 (2002), 305–308.

87. Helleseth T. and Kløve T., On group-theoretic codes for asymmetric channels, *Inform. Contr.* 49 (1981), 1–9.

88. Hoory S., Linial N., and Wigderson A., Expander graphs and their applications, *Bull. Am. Math. Soc.* 43 (2006), 439–561.

89. Horak P. and Kim D., 50 years of the Golomb–Welch conjecture, *IEEE Trans. Inform. Theory* 64 (2018), 3048–3061.

90. Howgrave-Graham N. and Joux A., New generic algorithms for hard knapsacks, In Gilbert H. (ed.), *Advances in Cryptology— EUROCRYPT 2010*, Lecture Notes in Computer Science 6110, Springer (2010), 235–256.

91. Huber M., Authentication and secrecy codes for equiprobable source probability distributions, In *2009 IEEE International Symposium on Information Theory*, IEEE Press (2009), 1105–1109.

92. Huber M., Combinatorial designs for authentication and secrecy codes, *Found. Trends Commun. Inf. Theory* 5(6), (2010), 581–675.

93. Impagliazzo R. and Zuckerman D., How to recycle random bits, In *30th Annual Symposium on Foundations of Computer Science*, IEEE Press (1989), 248–253.

94. Isaacs I. M., *Character Theory of Finite Groups*, Dover Publications (1994).

95. Jacobson D. and Williams K. S., On the number of distinguished representations of a group element, *Duke Math. J.* 39 (1972), 521–527.

96. Jones N. C. and Pevzner P. A., *An Introduction to Bioinformatics Algorithms*, The MIT Press (2004).

97. Jurafsky D. and Martin J. H., *Speech and Language Processing: An Introduction to Natural Language Processing, Computational Linguistics, and Speech Recognition*, third edition draft, https://web.stanford.edu/~jurafsky/slp3/ed3book.pdf (2018).

134 ■ Bibliography

98. Karloff H. J., Suri S., and Vassilvitskii S., A model of computation for MapReduce, In *Proceedings of the 21st Annual ACM-SIAM Symposium on Discrete Algorithms—SODA 2010*, SIAM (2010), 938–948.

99. Kelarev A., Ryan J., Rylands L., Seberry J., and Yi X., Discrete algorithms and methods for security of statistical databases related to the work of Mirka Miller, *J. Discrete Algorithms* 52/53 (2018), 112–121.

100. Kellerer H., Pferschy U., and Pisinger D., *Knapsack Problems*, Springer-Verlag (2004).

101. Kiani D. and Mollahajiaghaei M., On the addition of units and non-units in finite commutative rings, *Rocky Mountain J. Math.* 45 (2015), 1887–1896.

102. Kløve T., Error correcting codes for the asymmetric channel, Technical Report, Department of Informatics, University of Bergen, Norway (1995).

103. Kluyver J. C., Some formulae concerning the integers less than n and prime to n, *Proc. R. Neth. Acad. Arts Sci. (KNAW)* 9 (1906), 408–414.

104. Knuth D. E., *The Art of Computer Programming, vol. 2: Seminumerical Algorithms*, 3rd ed., Addison-Wesley (1997).

105. Koch R. D. M. and Ramgoolam S., Strings from Feynman graph counting: Without large N, *Phys. Rev. D* 85 (2012), 026007.

106. Koch R. D. M., Ramgoolam S., and Wen C., On the refined counting of graphs on surfaces, *Nuclear Phys. B* 870 (2013), 530–581.

107. Koiliaris K. and Xu C., Faster pseudopolynomial time algorithms for subset sum, *ACM Trans. Algorithms* 15 (2019), 40:1–40:20.

108. Kostov V. P. and Shapiro B., Hardy-Petrovitch-Hutchinson's problem and partial theta function, *Duke Math. J.* 162 (2013), 825–861.

109. Krawczyk H., LFSR-based hashing and authentication, In *Advances in Cryptology—CRYPTO '94*, Lecture Notes in Computer Science 839, Springer (1994), 129–139.

110. Krawczyk H., The order of encryption and authentication for protecting communications (or: How secure is SSL?), In *Advances in Cryptology—CRYPTO 2001*, Lecture Notes in Computer Science 2139, Springer (2001), 310–331.

111. Kulkarni A. A. and Kiyavash N., Nonasymptotic upper bounds for deletion correcting codes, *IEEE Trans. Inform. Theory* 59 (2013), 5115–5130.

112. Lagarias J. C. and Weiss B. L., Splitting behavior of S_n-polynomials, *Res. Number Theory* 1 (2015), Article 7.

113. Lando S. K. and Zvonkin A. K., *Graphs on Surfaces and Their Applications (with Appendix by D. B. Zagier)*, Springer-Verlag (2004).

114. Langley J. K., A certain functional-differential equation, *J. Math. Anal. Appl.* 244 (2000), 564–567.

115. Le T. A. and Nguyen H. D., New multiple insertion/deletion correcting codes for non-binary alphabets, *IEEE Trans. Inform. Theory* 62 (2016), 2682–2693.

116. Lehmer D. N., Certain theorems in the theory of quadratic residues, *Am. Math. Monthly* 20 (1913), 151–157.

117. Lehmer D. N., On the congruences connected with certain magic squares, *Trans. Am. Math. Soc.* 31 (1929), 529–551.

118. Leiserson C. E., Schardl T. B., and Lee I. A., *Cilk Hub*, http://cilk.mit.edu, MIT (2018).

119. Leiserson C. E., Schardl T. B., and Sukha J., Deterministic parallel random-number generation for dynamic-multithreading platforms, In *Proceedings of the 17th ACM SIGPLAN Symposium on Principles and Practice of Parallel Programming—PPoPP 2012*, ACM (2012), 193–204.

120. Lenz A., Siegel P. H., Wachter-Zeh A., and Yaakobi E., Coding over sets for DNA storage, *ISIT* (2018), 2411–2415.

121. Levenshtein V. I., Binary codes capable of correcting deletions, insertions and reversals (in Russian), *Doklady Akademii Nauk SSSR* 163 (1965a), 845–848. English translation in *Soviet Physics Dokl.* 10 (1966), 707–710.

122. Levenshtein V. I., Binary codes capable of correcting spurious insertions and deletions of ones (in Russian), *Problemy Peredachi Informatsii* 1 (1965b), 12–25. English translation in *Problems of Information Transmission* 1 (1965), 8–17.

123. Lidl R. and Niederreiter H., *Finite Fields*, 2nd ed., Cambridge University Press (1997).

124. Liebeck M. W. and Shalev A., Fuchsian groups, coverings of Riemann surfaces, subgroup growth, random quotients and random walks, *J. Algebra* 276 (2004), 552–601.

125. Liebeck M. W. and Shalev A., Fuchsian groups, finite simple groups and representation varieties, *Invent. Math.* 159 (2005), 317–367.

126. Liskovets V. A., A multivariate arithmetic function of combinatorial and topological significance, *Integers* 10 (2010), 155–177.

127. Liu Y., On some conjectures by Morris et al., about zeros of an entire function, *J. Math. Anal. Appl.* 226 (1998), 1–5.

128. Lovász L., Spectra of graphs with transitive groups, *Period. Math. Hungar.* 6 (1975), 191–195.

129. Lubotzky A., Expander graphs in pure and applied mathematics, *Bull. Am. Math. Soc.* 49 (2012), 113–162.

130. Lyubashevsky V., Palacio A., and Segev G., Public-key cryptographic primitives provably as secure as subset sum, In *Theory of Cryptography (TCC 2010)*, Lecture Notes in Computer Sceince 5978, Springer (2010), 382–400.

131. Manning C. D., Raghavan P., and Schütze H., *Introduction to Information Retrieval*, Cambridge University Press (2008).

132. Mans B. and Shparlinski I., Random walks, bisections and gossiping in circulant graphs, *Algorithmica* 70 (2014), 301–325.

133. Maze G., Partitions modulo n and circulant matrices, *Discrete Math.* 287 (2004), 77–84.

134. McAven L., Safavi-Naini R., and Yung M., Symmetric authentication codes with secrecy and unconditionally secure authenticated encryption, In *Progress in Cryptology—INDOCRYPT 2004*, Lecture Notes in Computer Science 3348, Springer (2004), 148–161.

135. McCarthy P. J., *Introduction to Arithmetical Functions*, Springer-Verlag (1986).

136. McEliece R. J. and Rodemich E. R., The Constantin–Rao construction for binary asymmetric error-correcting codes, *Inform. Contr.* 44 (1980), 187–196.

137. Mednykh A. and Nedela R., Enumeration of unrooted maps of a given genus, *J. Combin. Theory Ser. B* 96 (2006), 706–729.

138. Mednykh A. and Nedela R., Enumeration of unrooted hypermaps of a given genus, *Discrete Math.* 310 (2010), 518–526.

139. Mercier H., Bhargava V. K., and Tarokh V., A survey of error-correcting codes for channels with symbol synchronization errors, *IEEE Commun. Surv. Tutor.* 12 (2010), 87–96.

140. Metropolis N. and Rota G.-C., Witt vectors and the algebra of necklaces, *Adv. Math.* 50 (1983), 95–125.

141. Micciancio D., Generalized compact knapsacks, cyclic lattices, and efficient one-way functions, *Comput. Complexity* 16 (2007), 365–411.

142. Miller R. E., Thatcher J. W., Bohlinger J. D., and Karp M., Reducibility among combinatorial problems, In Miller R. E., Thatcher J. W., and Bohlinger J. D. (eds.), *Complexity of Computer Computations*, Springer (1972), 85–103.

143. Milnor J. and Thurston W., On iterated maps of the interval, In *Dynamical Systems*, Lecture Notes in Mathematics 1342, Springer (1988), 465–563.

144. Mitzenmacher M., A survey of results for deletion channels and related synchronization channels, *Probab. Surv.* 6 (2009), 1–33.

145. Montgomery H. L. and Vaughan R. C., *Multiplicative Number Theory I: Classical Theory*, Cambridge University Press (2006).

146. Motwani R. and Raghavan P., *Randomized Algorithms*, Cambridge University Press (1995).

147. Nagell T., Verallgemeinerung eines Satzes von Schemmel, *Skr. Norske Vid.-Akad. Oslo, Math. Class, I* 13 (1923), 23–25.

148. Nathanson M. B., *Additive Number Theory: The Classical Bases*, Springer-Verlag (1996).

149. Navarro G., A guided tour to approximate string matching, *ACM Comput. Surv.* 33 (2001), 31–88.

150. Nicol C. A. and Vandiver H. S., A von Sterneck arithmetical function and restricted partitions with respect to a modulus, *Proc. Natl. Acad. Sci. USA* 40 (1954), 825–835.

151. Nisan N., Pseudorandom generators for space-bounded computations. In *Proceedings of the 22nd Annual ACM Symposium on Theory of Computing—STOC 1990*, ACM (1990), 204–212.

152. Olson J., An addition theorem modulo p, *J. Combinatorial Theory* 5 (1968), 45–52.

153. Pagh A. and Pagh R., Uniform hashing in constant time and optimal space, *SIAM J. Comput.* 38 (2008), 85–96.

154. Planat M., Minarovjech M., and Saniga M., Ramanujan sums analysis of long-period sequences and $1/f$ noise, *Europhys. Lett. EPL* 85 (2009), 40005.

155. Rademacher H., Aufgabe 30, *Jber. Deutsch. Math.-Verein* 34 (1925), 158.

156. Ramanathan K. G., Some applications of Ramanujan's trigonometrical sum $c_m(n)$, *Proc. Indian Acad. Sci (A)* 20 (1944), 62–69.

157. Ramanujan S., On certain trigonometric sums and their applications in the theory of numbers, *Trans. Cambridge Philos. Soc.* 22 (1918), 259–276.

158. Razen R., Seberry J., and Wehrhahn K., Ordered partitions and codes generated by circulant matrices, *J. Combin. Theory Ser. A* 27 (1979), 333–341.

159. Rearick D., A linear congruence with side conditions, *Am. Math. Monthly* 70 (1963), 837–840.

160. Renner R. and Wolf S., Simple and tight bounds for information reconciliation and privacy amplification, In *Advances in Cryptology—ASIACRYPT 2005*, Lecture Notes in Computer Science 3788, Springer (2005), 199–216.

161. Ritchie R. and Bibak K., SQUAREMIX: A faster pseudorandom number generator for dynamic-multithreading platforms, In *Proceedings of the 2020 Data Compression Conference (DCC 2020)*, http://sigport.org/5068 (2020).

162. Rogaway P., Bucket hashing and its application to fast message authentication, In *Advances in Cryptology—CRYPTO '95*, Lecture Notes in Computer Science 963, Springer (1995), 29–42.

163. Rota G.-C., On the foundations of combinatorial theory. I. Theory of Möbius functions, *Z. Wahrscheinlichkeitstheorie und Verw. Gebiete* 2 (1964), 340–368.

164. Rudich S. and Wigderson A., *Computational Complexity Theory*, IAS/Park City Mathematics Series, American Mathematical Society (2004).

165. Ruskey F. and Sawada J., An efficient algorithm for generating necklaces with fixed density, *SIAM J. Comput.* 29 (1999), 671–684.

166. Sander J. W., On the addition of units and nonunits mod m, *J. Number Theory* 129 (2009), 2260–2266.

167. Sander J. W. and Sander T., Adding generators in cyclic groups, *J. Number Theory* 133 (2013), 705–718.

168. Sburlati G., Counting the number of solutions of linear congruences, *Rocky Mountain J. Math.* 33 (2003), 1487–1497.

169. Schardl T. B., Performance engineering of multicore software: Developing a science of fast code for the post-Moore era, PhD thesis, MIT (2016).

170. Schardl T. B., Lee I. A., and Leiserson C. E., Brief Announcement: Open Cilk, In *Proceedings of the 30th on Symposium on Parallelism in Algorithms and Architectures (SPAA '18)*, ACM (2018), 351–353.

171. Schardl T. B., Moses W. S., and Leiserson C. E., Tapir: Embedding fork-join parallelism into LLVM's intermediate representation, In *Proceedings of the 22nd ACM SIGPLAN Symposium on Principles and Practice of Parallel Programming (PPoPP '17)*, ACM (2017), 249–265.

172. Schoeny C., Wachter-Zeh A., Gabrys R., and Yaakobi E., Codes correcting a burst of deletions or insertions, *IEEE Trans. Inform. Theory* 63 (2017), 1971–1985.

173. Scholl P. and Smart N., Improved key generation for Gentry's fully homomorphic encryption scheme, In *Cryptography and Coding*, Lecture Notes in Computer Science 7089, Springer (2011), 10–22.

174. Schönemann T., Theorie der symmetrischen Functionen der Wurzeln einer Gleichung. Allgemeine Sätze über Congruenzen

nebst einigen Anwendungen derselben, *J. Reine Angew. Math.* 1839 (1839), 231–243.

175. Scott A. D. and Sokal A. D., The repulsive lattice gas, the independent-set polynomial, and the Lovász local lemma, *J. Stat. Phys.* 118 (2005), 1151–1261.

176. Serre J.-P., *Linear Representations of Finite Groups*, Springer-Verlag (1977).

177. Shannon C. E., Communication theory of secrecy systems, *Bell Syst. Tech. J.* 28 (1949), 656–715.

178. Shoup V., *A Computational Introduction to Number Theory and Algebra*, 2nd ed., Cambridge University Press (2009).

179. Siegel A., On universal classes of extremely random constant-time hash functions, *SIAM J. Comput.* 33 (2004), 505–543.

180. Sipser M., A complexity theoretic approach to randomness, In *Proceedings of the 15th Annual ACM Symposium on Theory of Computing (STOC 1983)*, ACM (1983), 330–335.

181. Sloane N. J. A., On single-deletion-correcting codes, In Arasu K. T. and Seress A. (eds.), *Codes and Designs: Proceedings of a Conference Honoring Professor Dijen K. Ray-Chaudhuri on the Ocassion of His 65th Birthday*, Walter de Gruyter (2002), 273–291.

182. Sokal A. D., The leading root of the partial theta function, *Adv. Math.* 229 (2012), 2603–2621.

183. Spilker J., Eine einheitliche Methode zur Behandlung einer linearen Kongruenz mit Nebenbedingungen, *Elem. Math.* 51 (1996), 107–116.

184. Stanley R. P., *Enumerative Combinatorics*, vol. 2, Cambridge University Press (1999).

185. Stanley R. P., *Enumerative Combinatorics*, vol. 1, 2nd ed., Cambridge University Press (2012).

186. Stanley R. P. and Yoder M. F., A study of Varshamov codes for asymmetric channels, Technical Report 32-1526, vol. XIV, Jet Propulsion Laboratory, California Institute of Technology, USA (1973), 117–123.

187. Steele, Jr. G. L., Lea D., and Flood C. H., Fast splittable pseudorandom number generators, In *Proceedings of the 2014 ACM International Conference on Object Oriented Programming Systems Languages & Applications (OOPSLA '14)*, ACM (2014), 453–472.

188. Stinson D. R., *On the connection between universal hashing, combinatorial designs and error-correcting codes, Congressus Numerantium* 114 (1996), 7–27.

189. Sun C.-F. and Yang Q.-H., On the sumset of atoms in cyclic groups, *Int. J. Number Theory* 10 (2014), 1355–1363.

190. Szemerédi E., Structural approach to subset sum problems, *Found. Comput. Math.* 16 (2016), 1737–1749.

191. Tabatabaei Yazdi S. M. S. and Dolecek L., A deterministic polynomial-time protocol for synchronizing from deletions, *IEEE Trans. Inform. Theory* 60 (2014), 397–409.

192. Thibon J.-Y., The cycle enumerator of unimodal permutations, *Ann. Comb.* 5 (2001), 493–500.

193. Tóth L., Some remarks on a paper of V. A. Liskovets, *Integers* 12 (2012), 97–111.

194. Tóth L., Counting solutions of quadratic congruences in several variables revisited, *J. Integer Seq.* 17 (2014), Article 14.11.6.

195. Tóth L. and Haukkanen P., The discrete Fourier transform of r-even functions, *Acta Univ. Sapientiae, Math.* 3 (2011), 5–25.

196. Tyagi H. and Vardy A., Universal hashing for information-theoretic security, *Proc. IEEE* 103 (2015), 1781–1795.

197. Vaidyanathan P. P., Ramanujan sums in the context of signal processing—Part I: Fundamentals, *IEEE Trans. Signal Process.* 62 (2014a), 4145–4157.

198. Vaidyanathan P. P., Ramanujan sums in the context of signal processing—Part II: FIR representations and applications, *IEEE Trans. Signal Process.* 62 (2014b), 4158–4172.

199. Varshamov R. R., On an arithmetic function with an application in the theory of coding (in Russian), *Dokl. Akad. Nauk SSSR* 161 (1965), 540–543.

200. Varshamov R. R., A class of codes for asymmetric channels and a problem from the additive theory of numbers, *IEEE Trans. Inform. Theory* 19 (1973), 92–95.

201. Varshamov R. R. and Tenengolts G. M., Codes which correct single asymmetric errors (in Russian), *Avtomatika i Telemekhanika* 26 (1965), 288–292. English translation in *Automation and Remote Control* 26 (1965), 286–290.

202. Vaughan R. C., *The Hardy-Littlewood Method*, 2nd ed., Cambridge University Press (1997).

203. Venkataramanan R., Swamy V. N., and Ramchandran K., Low-complexity interactive algorithms for synchronization from deletions, insertions, and substitutions, *IEEE Trans. Inform. Theory* 61 (2015), 5670–5689.

204. von Sterneck R. D., Ein Analogon zur additiven Zahlentheorie, *Sitzber, Akad. Wiss. Wien, Math. Naturw. Klasse* 111(Abt. IIa) (1902), 1567–1601.

205. Walsh T. R., Counting maps on doughnuts, *Theoret. Comput. Sci.* 502 (2013), 4–15.

206. Wang W. and Xia X.-G., A closed-form robust Chinese remainder theorem and its performance analysis, *IEEE Trans. Signal Processing* 58 (2010), 5655–5666.

207. Wegman M. N. and Carter J. L., New hash functions and their use in authentication and set equality, *J. Comput. System Sci* 22 (1981), 265–279.

208. Weisner L., Abstract theory of inversion of finite series, *Trans. Am. Math. Soc.* 38 (1935), 474–484.

209. Weiss A. and Rogers T. D., The number of orientation-reversing cycles in the quadratic map, In *Oscillation, Bifurcation and Chaos*, CMS Conference Proceedings8, AMS (1987), 703–711.

210. Wiman A., Üeber die hyperelliptischen Curven und diejenigen vom Geschlechte $p = 3$ welche eindeutigen Transformationen in sich zulassen, *Bihang Till. Kongl. Svenska Veienskaps-Akademiens Hadlingar, Stockholm* 21 (1895–1896), 1–23.

211. Yang Q.-H. and Tang M., On the addition of squares of units and nonunits modulo n, *J. Number Theory* 155 (2015), 1–12.

212. Zieschang H., Vogt E., and Coldeway H.-D., *Surfaces and Planar Discontinuous Groups*, Springer-Verlag (1980).

Index

Printed in the United States
by Baker & Taylor Publisher Services